Embark on a Journey
with Complete Tra~~ini~~~~ng~~

The Loveday Method®

The very first in the Series of
Seven Books.

The Loveday Method
Part 1

A Heptalogy
By
Geoffrey Loveday

MAPLE
PUBLISHERS

The Loveday Method Book 1

Author: Geoff Loveday

Copyright © Geoff Loveday (2024)

The right of Geoff Loveday to be identified as author of this work has been asserted by the author in accordance with section 77 and 78 of the Copyright, Designs and Patents Act 1988.

First Published in 2024

ISBN 978-1-83538-164-9 (Paperback)
       978-1-83538-165-6 (Hardback)
       978-1-83538-166-3 (E-Book)

Published by:
       Maple Publishers
       Fairbourne Drive, Atterbury,
       Milton Keynes,
       MK10 9RG, UK
       www.maplepublishers.com

Guidelines for Sharing the Knowledge of The Loveday Method

As you embark on the enlightening journey through this book, it's important to understand and respect the guidelines surrounding the dissemination of The Loveday Method. The insights and teachings provided here are for your personal and professional development. Please be aware that while you are encouraged to apply the knowledge gained for your own growth and practice, teaching or training others in The Loveday Method requires explicit permission. This policy ensures the integrity and quality of the method are maintained, and allows for a controlled and responsible spread of this valuable knowledge.

I wonder where life will take us now...

And the journey begins.

Let me take you on this magical adventure.

Contents

Dedication:

My beautiful and courageous wife;

This volume is more than a mere assemblage of words; it stands as a tribute to a woman of remarkable love and fortitude who left an indelible mark on the hearts of those she encountered. My extraordinary and valiant wife was taken from this world too soon, creating a gap that remains unfilled. Her children and I are reminded daily of our profound loss, with a persistent sorrow that commemorates the astonishing woman we had the privilege to know and cherish.

Despite the sorrow her absence brings, her spirit endures, offering ceaseless inspiration. She embodied the essence of living with bravery, compassion, and elegance. Her resilience in adversity, her selflessness, and her boundless love profoundly impacted everyone in her orbit. Her memory will continue to motivate us in all our endeavours.

This book is dedicated to my wife, a woman whose legacy of love and courage will perpetually reside in our hearts. While we may never completely recover from the agony of her loss, we find solace in knowing that her luminous presence still guides us through the most challenging moments of life.

My Family;

Also to my cherished parents and my wonderful brothers, who are no longer with us. They were my heroes, always inspiring me. Their belief in me, even in moments of self-doubt, means everything. My love for them transcends words.

I am also grateful to my grandparents, aunts, and uncles, whose influence has been pivotal in my journey.

A special mention to my in-laws, Alma and Leon, for welcoming me into their family as a son.

To my children, the beacons in my life: my lovely daughters, Shanna and Gema, and my wonderful sons, Rudi, Joshua, and Zak. Your presence has been my motivation in the toughest times. My love for you is immeasurable.

My sons-in-law, Marc and Richard, hold a special place in my heart for their kindness and spirit.

To my delightful grandchildren, Cali, Carter, and Ralphie, thank you for filling my life with joy. My love for you is boundless.

Most importantly, to my extraordinary wife, Jackie, whose life ended too soon. Her strength and love continue to guide me. I hope she sees the beauty and love she left behind in our children and grandchildren.

Jackie made the world brighter and is deeply missed. This book is a tribute to her legacy and the love we shared.

Inspiration

The development of the Loveday Method has been deeply inspired by the ground-breaking contributions of several key figures in the history of hypnotherapy.

These pioneers, through their innovative work and theories, have laid the foundations upon which the Loveday Method builds.

Franz Anton Mesmer (1734 - 1815): Mesmer introduced the concept of "animal magnetism" or mesmerism, setting the stage for the modern understanding of hypnotism.

Count Maxime de Puysegur (1751–1825): A disciple of Mesmer, Puysegur explored the trance state of somnambulism, expanding our understanding of the hypnotic states.

James Braid (1795 – 1860): Braid, the Scottish surgeon, coined the term "hypnotism" and was pivotal in transitioning its perception from mysticism to a psychological and physiological basis.

James Esdaile (1808 – 1859): Esdaile's use of mesmerism for anaesthesia in surgeries in India showed the practical application of hypnotism in pain control.

Sigmund Freud (1856 – 1939): Freud's early use of hypnosis and his development of psychoanalysis significantly influenced the psychological understanding and therapeutic approach to subconscious issues.

Emile Coue (1857 – 1926): Coue introduced the concept of optimistic autosuggestion, a form of self-hypnosis, emphasising the power of positive thinking in healing and self-improvement.

Milton H. Erickson (1901 – 1980): Erickson revolutionised hypnotherapy with his innovative, flexible, and creative techniques, impacting both the theory and practice of modern hypnotherapy.

Dave Elman (1900 – 1967): Elman's practical and efficient approach to hypnotic induction and his emphasis on the therapeutic uses of hypnosis have greatly influenced hypnotherapy training and practice.

The Loveday Method, inspired by these distinguished contributors, seeks to further the understanding of the human psyche and offer transformative therapeutic experiences, building on the rich legacy of these pioneers in hypnotherapy.

The Author

The Odyssey of Geoffrey Loveday

Hello, I am Geoffrey Loveday, a professional who has dedicated his life to the mysteries and healing powers of the human mind. My journey has been as a full-time professional hypnotherapist and a practitioner in pure-hypnoanalysis, complemented by my role as a Certified Hypnosis Instructor. Beyond these roles, I am the creator of Inherited Therapy and The Loveday Method, innovative approaches designed to heal and transform lives.

To my own astonishment, this path has led me to become an author of four books. My initial trio of works delves into the depths of the human psyche, exploring the profound effects of Transgenerational Trauma and illustrating how the therapies I've developed can bring healing to a world riddled with suffering.

However, a new inspiration struck me – the realisation of the immense potential within young minds. This revelation led me to write a children's book, a piece aimed at nurturing and developing the untapped possibilities in the youth.

As this journey of writing and exploration continued, I understood the need for a comprehensive guide on the methodologies I've created. Hence, I penned another book, entitled 'The Loveday Method'. This work is not just a book; it's a training manual, encapsulating the essence and application of The Loveday Method by the use of hypnosis, designed to educate and empower those who seek to understand and utilise this approach in their therapeutic practices.

Originally, I wrote "Are You Reliving Somebody Else's Life?" with therapists in mind, believing they would be the primary audience for its insights. However, it didn't take long to see that the book's content had a much wider appeal. The ideas and strategies I discussed were not just for professionals but could benefit everyone. With this realisation, I decided to make these concepts more accessible. I carefully selected the most crucial and impactful ideas from the book and integrated them into a new work; *The Loveday Method*.

Where it all began:

Imagine combining the unique style of the pre-talk with the powerful Elman induction method. To complete this mix, we add the Journey, made possible through the innovative Loveday Method. This blend of techniques isn't just a methodology; it's a pathway to unlocking the mind's profound potential in a straightforward and engaging way.

The Loveday Method's development is a fascinating blend of personal experiences, dreams, and the profound impact it has had on those who've used it.

The story begins:

The story begins with a transformative experience during a session with a client who had a deep-seated fear of being away from home.

In this session, he had an almost mystical experience where he felt transported back in time, emotionally connecting with an ancestor. This connection wasn't just visual; it was deeply emotional, allowing him to understand and reflect upon his current life challenges. This session was a turning point, as it demonstrated how deeply our present lives are intertwined with our ancestral past.

But the roots of The Loveday Method trace back even further, to a series of vivid dreams that I began having years earlier. In these dreams, a voice that seemed ancient and wise imparted a significant truth: our current suffering and pain are often echoes of our ancestors' experiences, continuing to influence us across generations.

This voice entrusted me with a significant mission: to bring this understanding to light and to offer healing not just on an individual level but to the ancestral lineages people carry within them.

Initially, I was sceptical. Sharing these dream experiences with others felt risky; I feared they might question my sanity. But the clarity and persistence of these dreams were undeniable. Over time, it felt as if I was being guided by an unseen force, leading me to understand and help my clients with a precision that seemed beyond my own capabilities.

Each client I worked with seemed to fit into a larger puzzle. It became clear that while I was the facilitator of this process, the wisdom and guidance, were coming from something much greater. Eventually, the voice in my dreams instructed me to name this unique method after my surname, and thus The Loveday Method was officially born.

However, I feel compelled to mention another crucial detail. Despite my initial hesitation, a client-turned-close friend suggested I name it after myself, proposing "The Loveday Method." This suggestion struck me as more than mere coincidence, leading to the formal adoption of the name "The Loveday Method." Thanks Mathew.

While the story of The Loveday Method might sound fantastical or hard to believe, the evidence lies in the profound transformations of those who have undergone this method. Clients often struggle to articulate the experience, but the impact is deeply felt – a profound and real change.

This journey from dreams to reality, weaving through personal experiences and ancestral connections, underpins The Loveday Method. It's not just a therapeutic technique; it's a journey that touches lives in profound and often unexpected ways, bridging the past and present to foster healing and understanding.

The Blueprint Emerges:

The Loveday Method represents an innovative strategy designed to empower individuals to break free from the unseen forces influencing their lives. Imagine gaining access to a specific area of the brain that allows individuals to navigate their mental landscape and connect with the emotions and experiences of their ancestors.

This method involves understanding the life events of our predecessors and how these stories have shaped our present circumstances, offering a chance to empathetically engage with and process these past experiences.

Distinguished by its ability to involve participants in the lived experiences of relatives such as grandparents, uncles, and aunts, The Loveday Method enables individuals to confront and release the traumas that have been passed down through generations. This approach facilitates the disruption of cycles that perpetuate the replication of our ancestors' lives, offering a path towards healing and transformation.

Closing Thoughts:

It seems that the Loveday Method offers a novel and potentially transformative approach to personal healing and growth. By enabling individuals to connect with and understand the emotional legacies of their ancestors, it provides a unique avenue for addressing and healing inherited traumas. This method not only emphasises the importance of acknowledging the past and its impact on the present but also promotes the idea of breaking potentially harmful cycles. It's a reminder of how deeply interconnected we are with our history and how understanding this connection can be a powerful tool for personal transformation and emotional liberation.

The Loveday Method: Complete Training.

Embark on a Journey of Mastery with Complete Training in

The Loveday Method.

In today's world, making a living has become increasingly challenging. The standard forty-hour workweek is no longer sufficient for many, with people finding themselves working upwards of 60 hours just to make ends meet. Essentials like food, heating, and mortgages have become more expensive as the cost of living continues to rise. Gone are the days when one could expect to work with a single company until retirement; job security is a relic of the past, leaving many in precarious positions when companies downsize or close.

However, imagine a different scenario. What if I told you that there's an alternative way to earn a living? Imagine the possibility of making £42,000 a year by working just 5 hours a week, all from the comfort of your own home. This isn't just a theoretical idea—it's a reality that I've proven through The Loveday Method. This method offers a transformative approach to earning a living, providing a lifeline in these challenging times.

"The most difficult moments are often the ones that force us to grow the most. Yet, it is exactly in this dark place where we discover who we are and what holds true value for us."

- *Geoffrey E Loveday*

If there is one thing in life I've learnt, it's that you must never give up. We learn from an early age when we first learn to walk that we walk, we fall, and we get back up again. So, life teaches us to get back up, and we must never give in despite our falls.

Welcome to the comprehensive training program in The Loveday Method. This course is meticulously designed to guide you through every aspect of this revolutionary approach, ensuring a deep understanding and practical mastery. Whether you're seeking to enhance your professional skills or embark on a new career path, this training offers the tools and insights necessary for profound success.

You will delve into the core principles, techniques, and applications of The Loveday Method, gaining the knowledge and confidence to apply these methods effectively. Prepare to transform your career and enrich your practice with the expertise you will gain from this complete training in The Loveday Method.

The use of Hypnosis:

In this book, you will discover the key to a fresh start and a new beginning. It's more than just a guide; it's a gateway to a new career path. This isn't just about finding a job; it's about embarking on a journey towards a fulfilling and prosperous career.

Embrace the opportunity to transform your professional life and step into a future brimming with potential.

Welcome to your new beginning.

Unlocking the Secrets of Generational Trauma with The Loveday Method

The Loveday Method is a ground-breaking approach, utilising advanced techniques to navigate the realms of consciousness and traverse back in time. This method facilitates access to dormant memories embedded within one's DNA, often the hidden culprits behind generational trauma. The objective of this innovative therapy is to address long-standing traumas entrenched in family histories, unravelling the enigmatic patterns woven into our genes and consciousness.

Explore the Wonders of the Subconscious

Imagine harnessing the power of your mind, coupled with the capabilities of The Loveday Method, to create a portal into the depths of your subconscious. Picture the extraordinary possibility of reconnecting with lost loved ones, engaging in profound conversations as if transcending the barriers of time and space. Envision seeing their faces once more, hearing their voices, and feeling their presence in an ethereal reunion. This method unlocks the boundless potential of your subconscious, offering unparalleled comfort, healing, and a sense of closure. The Loveday Method is not just a therapeutic tool; it's a gateway to transformative experiences, bridging the gap between the living and the memories of those who have passed, offering a unique opportunity for healing and connection.

Embarking on a Journey of Discovery:

Every place on Earth, even the most hidden parts of Africa, has been fully explored and mapped. This means we've run out of new physical places to discover.

But people always crave new discoveries, believing that this quest for the unknown is what moves us forward.

So, why not turn our curiosity inward? The human mind is still a vast mystery, full of unexplored potential and secrets. By trying to understand how we think, feel, and perceive the world, we could unlock new breakthroughs. This exploration could change how we see ourselves, improve medicine, and even how we connect with each other.

It's time to dive into the mysteries of the mind. Who knows what we might find?

The hidden lessons of life that we learn:

Every test and every challenge in life directs us on the right path. In my opinion, I feel we are not in control of our lives. You may disagree with me, but please read on; we never go in a straight line; life is like a map.

Life is so unpredictable; one moment you feel happy, the next life takes you down and pulls you back. Someone says something that upsets you, and you react instantly at that moment; guilt, regret, remorse, it hits you like a thunderbolt. After a while, you look back and can't remember the argument.

Isn't it amazing how we can affect the moods of other people we love without realising; how silly arguments can escalate and hurt others as well as ourselves; and how we often find it so difficult to let go of what we feel inside

The simple words "I'm sorry" can have a tremendous effect. Is it stupidity or stubbornness that stops you? But when you look back at what happened, was it really important? Does it really matter?

We have to be careful of what we say and the things that we do. What we do in our lives greatly impacts the people we love.

The mind is so powerful. Do we create our life as we live it, or was our life created before birth? I believe our life is planned somehow, and it takes us on the right path.

There are two things that we are sure of in life: that we are born and we die. It's what we do in-between that matters, and make no mistake; we are definitely here to learn. Everything in life is a lesson.

Sarah's magical story of true courage

"Once upon a time, in a quaint village nestled among rolling hills, there lived a lady named Sarah. Known for her kind heart and warm smile, Sarah had always been someone who loved to help others. For years, she worked in a job that was secure but unfulfilling, dreaming of a career that could ignite her passion and allow her to make a real difference in the world.

"Sarah's true passion lay in the mystical art of hypnosis. She was fascinated by the power of the mind and how hypnosis could unlock doors to healing and self-discovery. But embarking on this new path was not a decision she took lightly. As a single mother of two wonderful children, she knew any change would affect not just her life but theirs as well.

"One starlit night, Sarah sat by her window, gazing at the moon's soft glow, her mind swirling with thoughts of her future. It was then that she noticed a peculiar glimmer in her garden. Curious, she stepped outside and was greeted by a sight that took her breath away.

There, fluttering amongst her flowers was a tiny creature, glowing with an ethereal light.

"The creature introduced itself as Luna, a fairy who had been drawn to Sarah's home by her strong desire for change and her pure intent to help others. Luna listened intently as Sarah shared her dreams and fears about changing her career and the impact it might have on her family.

"Moved by Sarah's earnestness, Luna bestowed upon her a magical gift - a crystal pendant that shimmered with an inner light. This pendant, Luna explained, would not only enhance Sarah's natural abilities in hypnosis but also ensure that her journey would not adversely affect her beloved children. It was a symbol of courage, change, and protection.

"Emboldened by Luna's gift and words of encouragement, Sarah embarked on her new journey with renewed vigour. She studied the art of hypnosis, dedicating herself to mastering its techniques and understanding its profound impact on the human mind.

"As she delved deeper into her practice, Sarah discovered that she had a unique talent for connecting with people and helping them heal from within. Her reputation grew, and soon, individuals from far and wide sought her help, each finding peace and solace through her guidance.

"Despite her success, Sarah never lost sight of what was most important · her children. The magical pendant ensured that her new career never came at the cost of her family's happiness. Instead, it brought them closer, as her children saw their mother transforming lives and following her dreams.

"Years passed, and Sarah's name became synonymous with healing and hope. She had not only changed her own life but had touched the lives of countless others, proving that with courage, determination, and a little bit of magic, anything is possible.

"And so, under the watchful eyes of the moon and stars, Sarah continued her work, a beacon of light in the lives of those who sought her help, living a life filled with purpose, love, and enchantment."

Embracing Change
The Transformative Journey of Belief and Courage

The story that you have read about Sarah is a fascinating representation of personal development and transformation. It is emphasised by the themes of bravery, believing in oneself, and the pursuing of aspirations in spite of the difficulties that may be encountered. This narrative not only functions as a piece of literature that is intended to inspire and motivate readers, but it also functions as a metaphor for the reader's own self-improvement and transformation potential.

The structure of Sarah's journey—from a life defined by routine and responsibility to one enriched by purpose and the desire to help others—mirrors the journey that many individuals aspire to undertake. This transformation is catalysed by her encounter with Luna, a fairy who provides her with a crystal pendant. This moment symbolises the external validation of Sarah's dreams and the potential within her to achieve them. However, the true essence of the story lies in the realisation that the real power for change comes from within, not from magical artefacts or beings.

The integration of magical elements, such as the fairy Luna and the crystal pendant, serves to illustrate the concept that belief in oneself can unlock extraordinary capabilities and change. This aspect of the story is particularly effective because it resonates with the universal desire for external signs of validation or magical solutions to our struggles, while ultimately reinforcing the message that the true source of change is found within oneself.

Sarah's use of hypnosis as a tool for helping others—and in the process, herself—highlights the transformative power of empathy and the desire to make a positive impact on the world. This element of the story underscores the idea that personal fulfilment often comes from contributing to the well-being of others, and that skills and passions can be channels for significant change.

Call to action:

The story's invitation to the reader to see themselves in Sarah's journey is a powerful call to action. It encourages self-reflection on one's own dreams, fears, and the barriers that prevent movement beyond the comfort zone. The narrative suggests that, like Sarah, readers have the capacity to embark on their own journeys of transformation by harnessing the power of belief in themselves.

In conclusion:

Sarah's story serves as an allegory for personal growth, emphasising that courage, self-belief, and the pursuit of one's dreams are fundamental to achieving a life of purpose and joy. It invites readers to consider their own potential for transformation and to take the steps necessary to realise their dreams, reminding them that the magic required for change lies within their own hearts and minds. This tale, therefore, is not only about Sarah's metamorphosis but also a universal call to embrace the possibility of change in one's own life.

PART ONE

The understanding of

The Loveday Method

I wonder where life will take us now.

And so the journey begins.

So let me take you on this magical adventure.

The Hidden Lesson That Life Teaches Us.

As we embark on this journey of life, the path ahead is shrouded in mystery. It's as if we're on an enchanting quest, led by an unseen force. Each day presents a new test, nudging us toward our destined path. Our experiences are not just random events; they're lessons, shaping us even when they seem beyond our control. It's crucial to delve deeper and seek the messages life imparts.

Pause and reflect on your day. What lessons has it offered? What might you have done differently? Step back and contemplate your life's journey.

What is so different about the writings in this book? Everything you are about to read will make perfect sense to you.

This book you're about to read is unique; its insights will resonate deeply. I never imagined myself as a writer, yet here I am, driven by a belief that has transformed lives before my eyes. The joy and transformations I witness daily are not my doing alone; something greater is at work.

There's an urgent need to address the invisible force wreaking havoc on countless lives – not just the individuals directly affected but their families, friends, and future generations. This energy we absorb from others, like an infectious disease, is deeply ingrained, passed down even before our birth.

This book is a beacon of hope, offering tools to therapists and those struggling with depression, anxiety, stress, phobias, and fears. It tackles an invisible epidemic causing widespread misery. Where does this force originate? Are we misdirected in our search for answers? Perhaps these burdens we bear aren't ours but inherited from our ancestors, triggered later in life and influencing us in ways we're just beginning to understand.

What if you could journey back in time, live through your ancestors' experiences, and release the emotions you've inherited, addressing the root of these issues? The answers you seek are woven throughout this book, revealing secrets hidden within its pages.

Life's challenges have deepened my ability to connect with others, as I've faced numerous struggles myself. Over time, I've come to understand that our emotional responses, such as anger or resentment, might not solely stem from our personal experiences. Current scientific studies suggest that the impact of suffering can be inherited, passing through generations. The residue of pain, distress, and bitterness can persist, outliving those who first experienced them and echoing in the lives of their descendants.

The research I refer to was published in the journal "Science" in 2014, led by Dr. Rachel Yehuda and her team at the Icahn School of Medicine at Mount Sinai.

They discovered that children of Holocaust survivors who endured trauma were more prone to PTSD, indicating that trauma's effects can be hereditary.[1]

---

[1] Yehuda, R., Daskalakis, N.P., Lehrner, A., Desarnaud, F., Bader, H.N., Makotkine, I., Flory, J.D., Bierer, L.M. and Meaney, M.J. (2014). Influences of Maternal and Paternal PTSD on Epigenetic Regulation of the Glucocorticoid Receptor Gene in Holocaust Survivor Offspring. American Journal of Psychiatry, 171(8), pp.872–880.

This book aims to illustrate how trauma can travel through generations and how we, as professionals, can intervene to halt this perpetual cycle.

Grasping the concepts of epigenetics and transgenerational trauma unveils the reason behind the creation of The Loveday Method.

It also illuminates how, through the use of hypnosis, therapists can alleviate suffering worldwide.

Chapter 1: Exploring the Depths of Epigenetics.

Epigenetics and How It Affects Your Life
"The past explains how I got here, but the future is up to me."

Janice Dickinson

The Impact of Epigenetics on Your Existence
"Our history shapes our journey, but our choices forge our path ahead."

Geoffrey E Loveday

Let's ponder over a critical inquiry: What are the origins of these pervasive, dominant emotions?

To understand better, we delve into scientific studies and pose fundamental questions:

Is it plausible that emotional legacies are passed down through generations?

Might it be that the emotions influencing our present experiences — such as depression, anxiety, stress, fear, sadness, and loneliness — are echoes of our ancestors sentiments?

Are the emotional burdens we carry reflections of the lives of our ancestors, like great-great-grandparents, grandparents, and parents?

Are we inadvertently living through their experiences, and are we searching for answers in the wrong places?

Sir John Gurdon and Shinya Yamanaka earned them the Nobel Prize for Physiology or Medicine in 2012.[2]

Sir John Gurdon and Shinya Yamanaka, renowned as "Epigenetics Trailblazers", earned the Nobel Prize in Physiology or Medicine in 2012. This accolade was recognition of their ground-breaking contributions to our comprehension of diseases and development.

Their experiments revealed that differentiated somatic cells could be reverted to stem cells by altering gene expression without modifying the genomic sequence. This discovery underscored the role of

[2] https://www.nobelprize.org/prizes/medicine/2012/press-release/

epigenetic mechanisms in regulating gene expression at the cellular level.

Their findings not only illustrated the significant role of epigenetics in cell differentiation and its potential applications in regenerative medicine but also indicated that epigenetic alterations could be inherited across generations, influencing human health and disease.[3]

Reflecting on our life experiences, we recognise a transformation from our once innocent selves. Emotions like depression, sadness, guilt, fear, worry, and many others undeservedly infiltrate our thoughts. But where do these emotions originate?

[3] Surani, M. Azim (2012). Cellular Reprogramming in Pursuit of Immortality. Cell Stem Cell, 11(6), pp.748–750. doi:10.1016/j.stem.2012.11.014.

Rachel Yehuda

Rachel Yehuda / Icahn School of Medicine

For over 30 years, Dr. Rachel Yehuda,[4] a distinguished professor in Psychiatry and Neuroscience at the Icahn School of Medicine at Mount Sinai, has conducted extensive research into the psychological impacts of the Holocaust.

Renowned for her contributions to the study of trauma and Post-Traumatic Stress Disorder (PTSD), her ground-breaking work has shed light on how trauma affects gene expression, potentially influencing subsequent generations. This research underscores the likelihood of increased stress and mental health issues in the descendants of trauma survivors.

Dr. Yehuda's specific focus on the grandchildren of Holocaust survivors reveals the potential for inherited psychological trauma and stress, supporting her theory of epigenetic transmission of trauma across

---

[4] Yehuda, R., Daskalakis, N.P., Lehrner, A., Desarnaud, F., Bader, H.N., Makotkine, I., Flory, J.D., Bierer, L.M. and Meaney, M.J. (2014). Influences of Maternal and Paternal PTSD on Epigenetic Regulation of the Glucocorticoid Receptor Gene in Holocaust Survivor Offspring.

generations. Her findings raise profound questions about the origins of such inherited trauma and its historical depth.

The relationship between our genetic makeup and our emotional experiences remains an area of ongoing scientific exploration. Emerging research indicates that emotional inheritance might trace back to early childhood experiences.

For instance, studies show that babies in emotionally turbulent households may develop heightened physiological responses to their parents' emotional states, interpreting these emotions as signals of significant environmental changes.

Further research highlights that children in conflict-heavy homes may exhibit more aggressive behaviour, potentially linked to genetic factors like the MAOA gene, known to be partly inheritable.[5]

---

[5] Morris, A.S., Silk, J.S., Steinberg, L., Myers, S.S. and Robinson, L.R. (2007). The Role of the Family Context in the Development of Emotion Regulation. Social Development, [online] 16(2), pp.361–388.

These findings suggest a complex interplay between genetics and environment in shaping our emotional responses and behaviours from a very young age. While science is still evolving, it's clear that both inherited and environmental factors contribute significantly to our emotional development.

We are "programmed" from the moment we are born. When we learn to walk a programme is formed ,when we learn to read a programme is formed; when we learn to write a programme is formed; when we learn sadness a programme is formed; and when we learn fear a programme is formed.

Canadian psychologist Ron Hebb

On June 26th, 1949, Canadian psychologist Ron Hebb[6] published the article "On Seeing Things" in The American Psychologist.

In his paper, Hebb argued for a neurophysiological theory of perception and developed the hypothesis that "neurons that fire together will wire together". This theory is known as Hebb's rule, or "Hebbian" learning, and is one of the first scientific explanations of how learning occurs.

Before Hebb's paper, most psychologists believed that perception was a passive process in which the senses receive stimuli and then processed by the brain. Hebb argued that perception is an active process in which the brain constructs its representation of the world. His theory has been widely accepted and influential in cognitive psychology's development.

Hebb's theory was based on his observations of how neurons interact in the brain. He observed that when

---

[6] https://en.wikipedia.org/wiki/Donald_O._Hebb.

two neurons fire together, they become stronger and more likely to fire together in the future. Hebb hypothesised that this strengthening occurs because the neurons are connected via synaptic connections.

The theory has important implications for neuroplasticity because it provides a biological basis for the effect of the environment on specific behaviours, the main one being learning.

Hebb's theory explains how learning can occur at the cellular level and explains different types of learning, such as classical and operant conditioning. It can also explain why memory works.

Hebbian learning has helped develop models of perception, cerebellar function, and spatial mapping in the brain. A mathematical model of the neurons that implement Hebbian learning is called a Hopfield net. Researchers have used these nets to help design neural networks for tasks such as recognising the wiring together of neurons when hand-writing.

Ronald Hebb is considered to be one of the most influential psychologists of the 20th century. His theory of synaptic plasticity is one of the most widely-accepted theories in neuroscience. It has been used to explain various phenomena, from perceptual learning to memory formation. He was also a pioneer in the field of cognitive psychology

1.   What is Hebb's rule?

Hebb's rule indicates that neurons that fire together wire together. This means that when two neurons frequently activate simultaneously, the synaptic connection between them will strengthen, and learning can occur.

2.   How can Hebbian learning explain why memory works?

Hebbian learning can explain why memory works because it provides a biological basis for the effect of the environment on behaviour. This means that memories are not simply stored in the brain but are also shaped by our experiences.

3.   What are some of Hebb's other influential contributions to psychology?

Some of Hebb's other influential contributions to psychology include his explanation of how learning occurs and the invention of a mathematical model that implements Hebbian learning.

4.   Was Hebb involved in any other scientific fields?

Hebb contributed to neuroscience, cognitive psychology, and psychophysiology. Psychophysiology is the study of physiological responses to psychological processes and events.

5.   What awards did Hebb receive for his work?

He was awarded the Gold Medal for Meritorious Achievement in Psychological Science by the American Psychological Association and was inducted into the Canadian Medical Hall of Fame in 1995.

6.   When did Hebb die?

Hebb died in 1985.

Are We Reliving Someone Else's life?

Understanding of epigenetics and transgenerational trauma and The Loveday Method.

Regression with the Use of Hypnosis

Hypnosis is a powerful tool that can be used to help people understand and resolve past issues. Regression hypnosis involves going back in time to recall memories from earlier in life. This process can help people understand why they feel or behave a certain way, and it can also help them resolve any emotional issues that might be affecting their lives.

The regression use of Hypnosis can be used to help people become aware of past memories that they might not have known about consciously. This practice includes placing the client in a state of trance using various techniques, such as visualisations and guided imagery. Once the client is deeply relaxed, the therapist asks him or her to go back in time and explore memories from childhood or earlier.

The therapist will help the client understand the meaning of any memories revealed, and they will also work with the client to resolve any emotional issues associated with these memories. In addition, this process can benefit people struggling with emotional problems, such as anxiety or depression.

Regression use of hypnosis can also be used to help people resolve physical problems that might be related to past events. For example, a person might have a phobia linked to a past traumatic experience. Regression hypnosis can be used to help the person explore this experience and then resolve the trauma.

While it is rare, there are also some concerns about regression use of hypnosis. One risk is that a client might recall a memory suppressed due to extreme trauma or abuse. If this occurs, the therapist must be careful to handle the situation appropriately.

Past Life Regression with the Use of Hypnosis

One of the benefits of past life regression therapy is that it can be used as therapy for those suffering from persistent negative emotions.

As traumatic memories can be stored in the body, past life regression may help people process and release these emotions to feel more at peace with themselves.

In some cases, past life regression has been used to come to terms with the death of a loved one, as a person may have unfinished business with them.

Past life regression can also explore other spiritual beliefs, such as an individual's past lives and karmic patterns. For example, some researchers believe that past life regression therapy helps people come closer to their true selves.

In conclusion, although some people believe that past life regression therapy is a pseudoscience, it can be used as a form of therapy to help people process and resolve the negative emotions that they may carry around with them.

Inherited Therapy and The Loveday Method with the use of hypnosis

Inherited Therapy is a new approach to helping people release this invisible force controlling people's lives today.

Just suppose you could access a part of the brain and navigate through the mind to relive the feelings and emotions of our ancestors and experience what they felt and how their life's journey affects our life today and give them back.

To be able to take you on a journey where you will relive a moment in the first person as your grandfather, grandmother, uncles, or aunts and let go of the traumas you have been holding.

And that we are reliving someone else's life.

Understanding of Transgenerational trauma and The Loveday Method:

Refers to the profound and enduring impact of trauma that can span across multiple generations within families or communities. It occurs when the emotional, psychological, and cultural scars of traumatic experiences are passed down from one generation to the next.

This type of trauma can stem from a range of harrowing events, such as war, genocide, slavery, forced migration, natural disasters, and other forms of violence and oppression.

The consequences of this trauma become embedded in the descendants of those who initially endured it, often resulting in symptoms like anxiety, depression, post-traumatic stress disorder (PTSD), substance abuse, and various other mental and physical health challenges.

Recognising and addressing transgenerational trauma can be challenging because its effects may subtly influence individuals' lives and behaviours without an immediate connection to the historical trauma.

Nevertheless, understanding one's family or community history and experiences, coupled with seeking support from mental health professionals, can be pivotal in helping individuals and communities navigate the complex legacy of transgenerational trauma and promote healing and resilience.

Chapter 2: Inherited Therapy and The Loveday Method with the use of hypnosis

The Loveday Method represents an innovative methodology designed to assist individuals in liberating themselves from unseen forces that currently govern their lives.

Imagine the possibility of tapping into a specific area of the brain, enabling navigation through the mind's landscape to re-experience the emotions and feelings of our ancestors. This process involves understanding their experiences and the impact of their life stories on our present existence, allowing us to empathically return those experiences.

This therapeutic journey is unique, as it offers an opportunity to immerse oneself in the past experiences of relatives like grandparents, uncles, and aunts. Through this process, individuals can confront and release the traumas that have been unconsciously carried within them, effectively breaking the cycle of reliving the lives of those who came before us.

And that we are reliving someone else's life.

The Loveday Method presents a fascinating and innovative approach in the realm of hypnotherapy, to integrate elements of ancestral exploration and emotional healing focusing on the profound influence that the experiences and traumas of our ancestors can have on our current lives.

This method offers a unique therapeutic journey, allowing individuals to delve into the emotional and experiential narratives of their forebears, such as grandparents, uncles, and aunts, and to confront and release inherited traumas.

The method aligns with a growing understanding in psychology and therapy that our emotional and psychological makeup is not just shaped by our own experiences, but can also be significantly influenced by the histories and experiences of our ancestors.

This perspective acknowledges that family history, stories, and traumas can be passed down through generations, often unconsciously, influencing our behaviour, emotions, and life choices.

By providing a means to re‑experience and empathise with these ancestral emotions, the Loveday Method potentially offers a way for individuals to break free from repeating patterns and cycles that are not originally their own.

It's a therapeutic approach that appears to blend historical empathy, emotional release, and cognitive understanding to facilitate healing and personal growth.

This approach is intriguing and could represent a valuable contribution to the field of hypnotherapy, especially for those interested in the intergenerational transmission of trauma and the exploration of family histories as a means to understand and resolve current personal issues.

This new method developed will expand the boundaries of how we understand and heal the human psyche.

The stories in this book are about people who have faced difficulties and overcame them. They prove that it is possible to turn your life around, no matter how hard things may seem.

I hope their stories will inspire you to never give up on yourself and always to keep moving forward. And see how effective "The Loveday Method" is, and what you will be learning.

PART TWO

Their Stories

Rebecca's Story

Rebecca, an only child, had a difficult childhood marked by witnessing domestic violence and experiencing strict parental control. This caused her to be constantly cautious, creating a lasting impact on her life. As she grew older, she harboured feelings of anger towards her parents.

Tragically, she lost her mother at the age of 25, a loss deeply felt due to their close bond. Additionally, she lost her grandfather when she was 16 and both paternal grandparents. Rebecca approached me for help, struggling with depression, anxiety, and persistent feelings of unhappiness, sadness, and loneliness.

She is now ready to embark on a transformative journey towards healing, utilising a method known as The Loveday Method.

Rebecca's Magical Journey

"As I started this journey and the images started to appear I could see I was in a familiar environment, a place that reminded me of somewhere I'd been as a child, a space where I had good memories and felt safe. However this wasn't the same as reality, it wasn't my childhood of the 1990s, it was older, more basic, with less clutter. The space was almost barn-like and had a feel of being in the 16th or 17th century.

"I looked down and saw that I was a young woman wearing a well-worn dress, I was in my late teens. As I walked into the main room I felt a sense of calm. I'd gone to a place to reflect, a place of safety where I could look out of the window and watch people work on the fields as I processed my thoughts.

"This felt like a regular past-time, something I did whenever I could as respite from my life. I'd gone there to reflect on what felt like a huge turning point in my life, one I didn't want to take. I was due to be married to a much older local man who I was scared of, I didn't know him well, this marriage had been arranged by my father.

"I felt abandoned by my family, like they were just letting me go without a care and leaving me to become someone I didn't want to be. I felt trapped, like there was no way of getting out of it, nowhere to go. I was aware that even if I ran away and went somewhere else, I couldn't escape it.

"This was a societal expectation of my time, so I'd be judged and not be welcome in other communities. I felt immense sadness, fear and anticipation. Like life was never going to be the same again and my desire to make my own choices felt stronger than it was for other women of my age, as though I was someone who was meant for more than marriage and a quiet life, I felt disappointed and terrified of what life would bring.

"On reflecting, this journey makes me see the root of a number of challenges I have in my current life. I have regular anxiety about losing the life I have at the moment, the security of my family, my job, my home. I feel I'm successful in all these areas, and people are often shocked that I spend time worrying about this.

"I feel like my income, my husband or my son are going to be taken away at any time and often realise I'm looking for clues to justify my worries. In addition, I also have a real hatred of controlling men; my husband is calm and lets me live my life how I want to.

"However, I see friends with controlling partners or men in the workplace or my social life who are dominant and they make me angry and incredibly resistant to engaging with them.

"I've always wondered where this deep sense of anger comes from often putting it down to being a feminist, or being strong, but this journey has really made me think about that young girl, and see that both of these ways of being in my current life, link back to a scared person who had no way of escaping a foregone conclusion of her life path, one that had been decided by others."

Please read that again: Her life path was one that had been decided by others. Makes you think doesn't it?

The Loveday Method

Student: Mr Brian Folkard.

My name is Geoffrey Loveday, the founder of Inherited Therapy and The Loveday Method.

Today, I want to highlight Brian's extraordinary qualities, not just as an incredible human being who genuinely cares, but also as a skilled practitioner.

I trained Brian in a unique method, enabling him to assist every individual he encounters effectively.

While I don't often give reviews, Brian's exceptional ability to heal the mind of anyone who seeks his help compels me to share my experience and commend his expertise.

Deb's Mystical Adventure in the Cave

As guided by Geoff my next session of hypnosis will be again with Deb. This is the 4th session with Deb, known as the TREASURE MAP. Session was Monday 1st Aug 2022.

First thing I noticed when arriving was that Deb was obviously calm and relaxed and in her words "looking forward to the session".

Induction;

On settling Deb in the chair I use for hypnosis sessions and asking the question of touch being used on the hand, elbow, shoulder and forehead to be okay and confirmed. The induction begins.

Geoff's choice of induction is Elman. Now very conscious of this induction and much practised by myself, I feel confident in its effectiveness.

The above shows as Deb goes deep into hypnotic trance as shown by her body language.

Place of safety;

On completion of the induction, this is a method of focussing the client's attention on the hypnotist's voice and not allowing a separation from it during the session. This also is a deepener and a means to assure the client of safety. Finally to assist therapy suggestions nothing said should be deemed ridiculous or absurd.

Hands rising;

A technique developed to promote acceptance of past events and emotions and the realisation of not requiring to hold onto them. This also gives a way forward in knowledge of a great future ahead, a notable adventure.

A fascinating technique, this is fully explored and taught by Geoff.

At this point the journey purpose is suggested.

Deb is always upset about not being able to lose weight. I suggest an old map lost for centuries needs to be found to guide her to an answer to the question she is always asking.

Deb was guided on a magical journey when she stumbled upon a hidden cave with an old staircase. It looked a bit scary, but Deb was curious. So, she started climbing up.

With each step, Deb felt a mix of excitement and nervousness. She took a moment to breathe and gather her courage. Up ahead, there was a mysterious door and a cosy chair beside it. Deb pushed the door open and found herself in a grand hallway with beautiful chandeliers.

On a table, there was an ancient map. Deb looked at it closely and felt it guiding her to another staircase. This one was colourful and seemed to spiral down forever.

As she went down, something magical happened. Deb turned into a light and floaty version of herself, like a cloud! She was surrounded by bright colours and saw a kind, glowing figure.

In this dreamy world, Deb heard whispers of 'LEVITICUS' and saw a banner saying 'WE ARE NOT NEPHILIM.' The name 'JESUS' echoed around, filling her with happiness and love.

Soon, it was time to go back. Deb walked up the stone steps, counting them. When she opened her eyes, she was back in the real world, feeling joyful and thankful for such a wonderful adventure.

Closing thoughts;

In conclusion, Deb's magical journey serves as a metaphorical exploration of the human condition, reflecting our innate desire for exploration, the transformative power of discovery, and the eternal quest for spiritual understanding. It reminds us that within the mysteries of the universe lies the potential for profound personal growth and enlightenment, accessible to those who seek it with an open heart and a curious spirit.

Eddy's Journey

Ed came to see me for his first session beyond the pre talk during September 2023.

Noted was his problem with his current relationship which he wanted to rescue on his part knowing that his lack of focus and problems from a past relationship were holding him back.

The first session with me saw Ed go back to his childhood. At a point when 8-year-old Ed and his sister witnessed yet another argument between Mum and

Dad, feeling angry and scared, this feeling had remained with him.

Utilising the Loveday method this whole scene was turned around and the negativity from it released. Showing now the good times in his childhood including, the first time he walked, which was on grass in a park with family around, his 1st birthday and at age 6 playing with friends.

Eddie was now guided to a wonderful and tranquil valley. A place where he now met his nan who had departed this world when in his early teens. Nothing was said but Ed had a feeling of love and comfort knowing she was with him.

In closing:

Eddie noted to me that at the end of the program of 6 sessions, how each one had felt so uplifting, especially session 2, which gave release from a previous relationship that was stopping him from moving forward in this one.

Meeting friends and family and ancestors during these sessions allowed a belief in himself and in his words, I've now become a more positive and focussed person, which was my goal.

Contacted by Eddie early January 2024 to OK this transcript, it was joyful to hear that his relationship is flourishing and that he is a far happier person within himself.

What an amazing story.

Samantha's Story

Nightmares:

It's strange how some things happen to push you further into the path you should be on.

During an unexpected encounter with a professional counsellor, we discussed how hypnotherapy might benefit one of their clients. I decided to pursue this approach and began working with the counsellor's client, Samantha, a 24-year-old who had been receiving counselling for a while.

Previously, Samantha tried hypnotherapy six months earlier, but it hadn't made a difference in her situation. However, after a preparatory discussion that boosted my confidence and eagerness, we decided to try hypnotherapy again.

Samantha had been plagued by recurring nightmares of abuse since she was 5 until she was 7 years old, ceasing only when her abuser, her uncle, passed away. In our first hypnotherapy session, using the Loveday method, Samantha revisited these traumatic memories.

She was able to reshape these scenes, replacing them with happier moments, such as having a picnic with her boyfriend and taking selfies in front of the Eiffel Tower in Paris.

In this safe mental space, Samantha could confront an image of her uncle. She expressed her pent-up emotions, symbolically releasing them by striking a pillow. This aspect of the Loveday method proved particularly effective.

Samantha also addressed unresolved feelings towards her father, who she felt had not been the best parent. She imagined bringing him into this safe space and returning the negativity she felt towards him, thus liberating herself.

Guided to recall moments of unconditional love, such as her first steps, her first birthday, and being held by her mother, Samantha experienced these memories vividly through the Loveday Method.

The session culminated in a visualisation where Samantha found herself in a serene valley, met by her great-grandmother. This figure of love placed her hand on Samantha's head in a healing gesture, and after five minutes, Samantha nodded, signalling the completion of the process.

Upon returning to consciousness, Samantha's face was lit with a beautiful smile, and she expressed feeling wonderful.

A follow-up call three days later revealed that she had not experienced any nightmares since the session and was looking forward to the remaining sessions in our program.

In closing:

The experience with Samantha highlights the transformative power of hypnotherapy when combined with traditional counselling. It underscores the importance of exploring alternative therapeutic methods, especially for those who have struggled to find relief through conventional approaches.

Samantha's journey, from being haunted by traumatic childhood experiences to finding a sense of peace and healing, serves as a testament to the resilience of the human spirit and the potential for recovery.

This case also illustrates the critical role of a tailored approach in therapy. The use of the Loveday method, a technique that enabled Samantha to revisit and reshape her traumatic memories, proved crucial in her healing process.

It allowed her to confront and release deep-seated emotions in a safe and controlled environment, demonstrating how specific therapeutic techniques can be pivotal in addressing individual needs.

Moreover, Samantha's story is a reminder of the interconnectedness of our past experiences and present well-being. By addressing and resolving past traumas, individuals can significantly improve their current quality of life, as seen in Samantha's cessation of nightmares and her newfound sense of optimism.

In conclusion, Samantha's journey through hypnotherapy emphasises the power of compassionate, individualised care and the potential of alternative therapeutic methods to bring about profound and lasting change in individuals' lives.

Her progress is not just a success for her as an individual, but also a beacon of hope for others facing similar struggles, highlighting the endless possibilities for healing and growth.

Johnathan's Story

A Journey through Time: Revisiting Childhood with Geoff

"My first meeting with Geoff was like a trip back in time to my happy childhood days. We imagined walking up stairs to a door that opened to a path leading to a beautiful lake surrounded by trees. By the lake, I saw my dad, who I lost 13 years ago.

"It felt so real, seeing him there, telling me everything will be okay and that I'll have a long and happy life. It was so special to see him again, smiling and full of love, just as I remember.

"Then I walked back, through the door, to where Geoff was. This experience with Geoff was really something I'm thankful for.

"Thanks a lot, Geoff.

- Johnathan"

What Have we learnt:

Johnathan's recounting of his first meeting with Geoff unfolds as a poignant narrative that beautifully illustrates the profound impact of revisiting cherished memories, particularly those associated with childhood and lost loved ones.

This experience, marked by an imaginative journey to a serene lakeside setting, serves not only as a bridge to the past but also as a source of comfort and reassurance about the future.

The metaphorical ascent up the stairs and through a door leading to a path by a beautiful lake encapsulates the journey inward to the depths of one's memories and emotions.

The vivid imagery of the natural surroundings—a lake enveloped by trees—evokes a sense of peace and tranquillity, creating a perfect backdrop for the heartfelt reunion that follows.

Seeing his father by the lake, a figure of warmth, love, and guidance, despite having lost him 13 years prior, highlights the enduring presence of loved ones in our memories and the profound impact they continue to have on our lives.

His father's reassurance transcends the boundaries of time and space, offering Johnathan a message of hope and the promise of a fulfilling life ahead. This moment is not just a reflection on past happiness but also a profound emotional healing, providing Johnathan with a sense of closure and peace.

The return journey through the door, back to where Geoff was, symbolises the transition from the realm of memory and emotion back to the present reality, enriched by the experience.

This encounter, facilitated by Geoff, underscores the power of connection and shared experiences in uncovering deep emotional truths and fostering healing.

Johnathan's expression of gratitude towards Geoff for this experience is a testament to the transformative power of revisiting cherished childhood memories. It highlights the significance of such moments in providing comfort, healing past wounds, and offering guidance for the future.

Through this journey, Johnathan is reminded of the enduring love and wisdom passed down from his father, elements that continue to shape his life and outlook.

In closing:

Johnathan's experience with Geoff illuminates the intricate tapestry of human memory and emotion, revealing how revisiting the past can serve as a powerful means of understanding ourselves and navigating the complexities of life.

It is a reminder of the timeless bond we share with those we have lost and the healing power of love and memory.

Barry's Story

The power of love

First session was mind blowing. I felt like I fell into a hypnotic state quite easily. The first part that I remember was meeting my nans and Grandads. Nanny Pat came through first, the only words that were spoken was 'I love you'.

I wished I could have had a conversation but I think the only thing that ever mattered was love. That was actually the only thing that was present, just pure love.

Her brothers and sisters were all there too. All with smiles on their faces. I can't remember if I saw Grandad Bernie but I think he was there. Then Nanny Hazel and Grandad Wally came up. They were smiling too and the same loving feeling was present. It was such a beautiful experience.

The way my mind works can be very negative about any situation so this reminded me that when you strip everything back that it's only pure love that exists. I'm so grateful for my family, I know they love me.

The next thing I remember is that Geoffrey took me back to my first steps. After recalling who was there (Mandy and Paula) and a conversation with my mum and she confirmed they were there which absolutely blew my mind.

It made me feel like it's bull shit and I felt what I felt. I remember feeling awkward when I saw them in the room. Like I felt uncomfortable. I feel like I've always felt uncomfortable around them.

There was another moment when I found myself back in my mum's womb and I felt her stress. The hypnotist asked if I could feel anything else and obviously the presence of love was there. However there was always an underlying stress feeling.

My mum suffered a lot of stress during her pregnancy as her mum and dad were getting divorced, and the family suffered a lot of deaths one after another. So as a child being carried inside of a person with a huge amount of stress it makes sense that an unborn child is going to feel this too then probably carry it with them their whole lives and not understand why.

During my other sessions I had experiences with relatives and people I'd never met before. Some people I recognised for example my great grandparents showed up, my grandpa lost his dad during the war when he was 5 and his mother spent most of life in mourning for her husband to which I was shown in one of visions the deep sadness that surrounded my family. This experience was quite difficult for me and the feeling stayed with me for a few days.

My last session was the most profound, as I wanted to do hypnosis to stop smoking. Geoff told me I was going to meet my guardian angel and next thing I know I'm back in my nans (my dad's mum) living room, also this vision was different from the last experience I had with grandparents because I could actually feel the energy of her home.

All the smells of the house were there, I could smell breakfast being cooked, I could feel the warmth of the house and I could see her standing in front of me so clearly. We chatted and she put all my cigarettes in an old box and took them away from me. It was bitter sweet as she didn't come back but I remained in the living room with a feeling of pure contentment.

Since having hypnosis I've completely cut back on smoking, I have the feeling of completeness, I'm happier and don't suffer from any anxiety or depression any more, I actually like myself now and my outlook has completely changed. This has honestly been life changing for me

What have we learned:

Barry's journey through hypnotherapy appears to have been a deeply transformative experience, revealing several key insights and lessons.

The Power of Love: Barrie's initial experience with his departed grandparents highlighted the overarching presence and importance of love. Despite the lack of conversation, the feeling of pure love was dominant, suggesting that love is a fundamental and enduring element in human relationships.

Validity of Memories and Feelings: The revelation that his first steps were witnessed by specific people, later confirmed by his mother, validated his memories and feelings. This experience challenges scepticism and supports the idea that our subconscious mind holds accurate, deep-seated memories and emotions.

Impact of Prenatal Experiences: Finding himself in his mother's womb and sensing her stress during pregnancy illustrates how prenatal experiences can profoundly affect an individual. This suggests that the emotional state of a pregnant mother can imprint on the child, potentially influencing their emotional health and behaviour later in life.

Family History and Emotional Legacy: Encounters with relatives and learning about his family's history, especially the grief and sadness due to war and loss, indicate how family histories and emotions can be passed down through generations. This insight emphasises the importance of understanding and processing familial emotional legacies.

Healing and Closure: The session where Barrie's grandmother helped him with his smoking habit shows hypnosis's potential for practical, therapeutic outcomes. The vivid sensory experience and symbolic action of taking away the cigarettes indicate a deep psychological processing and a step towards healing and closure.

Personal Transformation: The overall impact of the hypnotherapy sessions on Barrie's life is significant. He reports a reduction in smoking, an increase in feelings of completeness and happiness, and a decrease in anxiety and depression. This transformation suggests that exploring and addressing subconscious memories and emotions through hypnosis can lead to profound personal growth and improved mental health.

Self-Acceptance and Positive Outlook: Finally, Barrie's newfound self-liking and changed outlook on life underscore the role of hypnotherapy in fostering self-acceptance and a positive perspective. This shift is crucial for overall well-being and can be a powerful outcome of therapeutic interventions like hypnosis.

In closing:

Barrie's journey through hypnotherapy highlights the profound impact of exploring and understanding one's subconscious mind. His experiences underscore the importance of emotional connectivity, the deep-seated influences of family history, and the transformative power of addressing past experiences.

This journey led to significant personal growth, healing, and a positive shift in his mental health and outlook on life, demonstrating the potential of such therapeutic approaches for personal empowerment and well-being.

The Sinking of the Lusitania.

This story is from my third book, "Is It Possible To Communicate With The Dead?"

My aim is to demonstrate the effectiveness of this method.

An interesting story. Where do I begin?

Jonathan came to see me on the 7th of January 2023 suffering from depression, anxiety, stress, unhappiness, and guilt.

He is 66 years young, happily married, and has two children and one granddaughter.

The guilt that he has is related to travelling away from home. I asked him if he had one wish, what would it be?

His answer was to enjoy his holiday. It seems so silly, doesn't it? But to him it wasn't, as it was affecting his life, and not only his, but the relationship with his family.

Every time they went away they would always have to come back early because he would have pains in his chest and panic attacks that became so severe they had to return home.

For every problem, there is a solution. We just have to find it.

The big question is where do we look for the answers?

I believe that the answers we are searching for were there long before Jonathan was born. That he was suffering from Transgenerational Trauma.

Transgenerational Trauma is a form of psychological trauma that is passed down from one generation to the next.

So how is it possible that something that happened 100 years ago, or 200/300/1000 years ago is causing the problem in Jonathan's life today and that he is reliving his ancestor's life?

Hopefully, I may give you an insight into why and how this is possible.

Let me drift away from the story just for a moment. And I would like to ask the readers a question.

Q. Would you believe that something that happened 100, 200, 500,1000, or 10000 years ago is affecting your life today?

I know it is difficult to believe. But bear with me for the moment. We know that cancer, diabetes and heart disease can be passed down from one generation to the next.

What about the misery, anxiety, and despair that our parents' great, great, grandparents experienced in their lives? Is it possible that we are holding onto their suffering?

Q. Who do you look like, your mum or your dad?

There will be similarities because your DNA is passed down from your parents to you. What about your grandparent's DNA is it also passed down from your grandparents to your parents to you, or your great-grandparent's DNA from your grandparents to your parents to you?

Epigenetics states it can go back over at least 14 generations. But do we really know how far it can go back?

There is an invisible force that is causing so much unhappiness in the world today; it is causing depression, anxiety, stress, fear and many other issues.

It is an epidemic affecting many people worldwide who have no idea where to get help.

And so The Loveday Method was formed.

The Loveday Method is a sophisticated means of achieving time travel through the mind in order to access hidden memories within the DNA responsible for generational trauma in order to unlock the shackles your ancestral traumas hold over you.

And that you are Reliving Someone Else's Life.

I encourage you to explore my website and view the video provided to gain a better understanding:

www.inheritedtherapy.com

Now let us get back to Jonathan's story...

It starts with me putting Jonathan into a very deep trance. I take him to the Akashic library, the library of life. In the library, there are many books he talks to me under hypnosis explaining exactly what he sees.

He tells me he sees a chair, a very old red leather chair he described in detail. I get him to sit in the chair and tell him that he will be transported through time to many generations before he was born where he will relive an ancestor's life whether it will be male or female, and where the fear that Jonathan is holding onto originated.

Once sitting in the chair it took him back to 1915, he became his great-great-grandfather, and he then explained to me in detail the experience he was feeling and reliving.

He told me he was dressed in a sailor's uniform and was looking forward to seeing his family who he missed so much.

He was sad that he had been away from home and his family for far too long and was depressed because of it.

He told me the date was May 1st 1915, and he was on pier 54, travelling from New York to Liverpool on the Lusitania.

The RMS Lusitania was a UK-registered ocean liner that made regular trips across the Atlantic at the time.

Unbeknown to him, he will never see his family again. On the 7th of May 1915, the Lusitania was torpedoed by an imperial German navy U-boat during the First World War and sunk just 11 nautical miles from Ireland.[7]

He then described to me his last moment. It is May 7th 1915; mid-afternoon, so I am looking forward to seeing his family. He tells me he's a stoker and he maintains the steamship's furnace.

His final memories are of the ship filled with water and the anguish he felt at not being able to see his family again.

[7] https://en.wikipedia.org/wiki/The_Sinking_of_the_Lusitania

At that moment I separated Jonathan from his great-great-grandfather and told him what to say. These words were:

'I will honour your memories, but I can't and won't hang onto your misery any longer; all the agony, suffering, and unhappy feelings you had in life are not mine. It's unfair that I should shoulder the burden of your feelings of shame and remorse, and your inability to overcome the feeling of never wanting to leave home.

They are not mine, they are yours, and I must give them back to you.'

At that moment, the dark energy left Jonathan and entered his great-great-grandfather, which also released his traumas, sadness, and fears, as it's something he doesn't deserve to have. That moment a beautiful golden light fell down from the universe and surrounded them both with love and light.

He looked into his great-great-grandfather's eyes and saw love, relief and inner peace. His great-great-grandfather entered a doorway of light, looked back and smiled as he stepped through into the light.

You see they were both trapped in a doorway of time and they could not move on. You just can't imagine what his great-great-grandfather must have been going through.

After the session, I'm happy to report that Jonathan's fear of being away from home has been overcome. He now goes on holiday with his family, and they travel all over Europe. His wife reached out to me, expressing her gratitude for helping her husband.

In closing:

You see they were both trapped in a doorway of time and they could not move on. I hope you the reader can now see the connection between that life and this life and the need for Jonathan to get home. And that he was reliving someone else's life.

PART THREE

The Loveday Method: The Training

To fully grasp and apply the wealth of knowledge this book offers, it is crucial to engage in a repeated and thorough reading process. This is not merely about skimming through the pages multiple times but involves a deep and reflective examination of its content.

With every read, layers of new information and insights are revealed, ones that might have been overlooked during the original reading of the material.

This step-by-step way of reading is essential. for developing a comprehensive understanding of the book's teachings. It enables the reader to connect with the material on a deeper level, with varied thoughts and complicated ideas that were not immediately obvious at first glance.

By dedicating time and effort to revisit the book's chapters, the reader embarks on a journey of continuous learning and discovery, thereby unlocking the full potential of the knowledge contained within its pages.

I'm thrilled to have you embark on this incredible journey with us. Today marks the beginning of a fascinating exploration into hypnosis, and I'm excited to guide you through it.

We have structured the training into various modules, each varying in length – this structure is designed to provide a comprehensive understanding of hypnosis and its applications, allowing for both insight and personal development.

As we commence, we'll start by sharing and dive into our first session. Today's training will cover several key aspects:

- Embark on a Journey of Mastery with Complete Training in "The Loveday Method"

- Inherited Therapy and The Loveday Method

- Raising the bar to a higher standard of excellence.

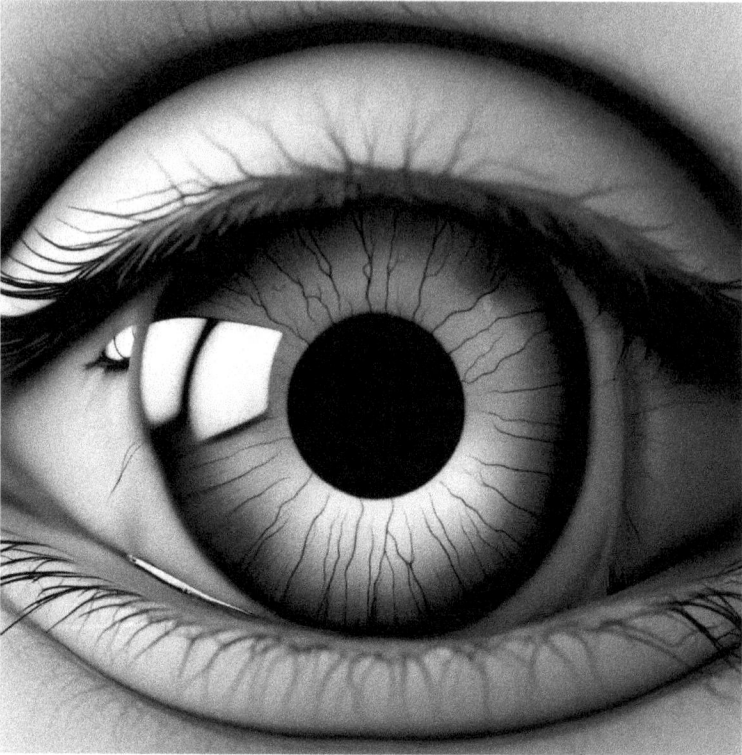

What your training will consist of:

Module 1: What is hypnosis?
Module 2: History of hypnosis
Module 3: Hypnosis Timeline
Module 4: Theory of the mind
Module 5: Brainwave States
Module 6: Belief in yourself
Module 7: Esdaile State: Hypnotic Coma
Module 8: Abreaction
Module 9: H+
Module 10: The Three Section Process
Module 11: The Pre-Talk
Module 12: Inductions

Module 13: Explanation: Instant Induction
Module 14: Hypnoidal Five and Signs of Trance
Module 15: Analytical Vs Non Analytical
Module 16: Types of Inductions (Instant and Rapid)
Module 17: Boilerplate 1
Module 18: Fractionation and Deepeners
Module 19: Post Hypnotic Suggestion
Module 20: Bring them back
Module 21: Regression
Module 22: Complete session: Regression
Module 23: Complete session: Suggestion therapy
Module 24: Induction for children
Module 25: Sleep Hypnosis: Dave Elman
Module 26: Techniques
Module 27: Survey Literature
Module 28: The Universe
Module 29: Working with adults: The Journey an adult will go on
Module 30: Working with children: The Journey a child will go on

This is just the beginning. Over the coming weeks, you will gain extensive knowledge and practical skills in hypnosis.

Let's embark on this exciting journey and dive into Module One!

Module 1: What is Hypnosis?

"Hypnosis is a state of special awareness and receptiveness to ideas...a special willingness to examine ideas for their inherent worth. The hypnotic state is a state in which the client pays attention to which is very important."

- Milton Erickson

"It is recognised that there is no generally accepted definition of hypnosis, though considerable consensus exists at a descriptive level."

- Martin T. Orne

"Hypnosis is control of thought and action through suggestion."

- Leslie LeCron

"Hypnotism is simply exaggerated suggestibility."

- George H. Estabrooks

"Hypnosis is a deep involvement and almost total immersion in an activity in one or more imaginative feeling areas of experience."

- Josephine Hilgard

"The greatest discovery of my generation is that human beings can alter their lives by altering the attitudes of their minds."

- William James

Chapter Summary: Understanding Hypnosis

In this module, we've learned the following key points in a straightforward manner:

Milton Erickson

"Hypnosis is a state of special awareness and receptiveness to ideas...a special willingness to examine ideas for their inherent worth."[8]

Key Idea: Hypnosis involves focused attention and openness to ideas.

Martin T. Orne

"There is no generally accepted definition of hypnosis, though there is considerable consensus at a descriptive level."[9]

Key Idea: Hypnosis is broadly understood, even without a precise definition.[8]

Leslie LeCron

"Hypnosis is control of thought and action through suggestion."[10]

Key Idea: Suggestion plays a central role in influencing thoughts and actions in hypnosis.

George H. Estabrooks

---

[8] https://en.wikipedia.org/wiki/Milton_H._Erickson
[9] https://en.wikipedia.org/wiki/Martin_Theodore_Orne
[10] LeCron, Leslie M. (1892-1972) | Encyclopedia.com

"Hypnotism is simply exaggerated suggestibility."[11]

Key Idea: Hypnosis enhances a person's natural suggestibility.

Josephine Hilgard

"Hypnosis is a deep involvement and almost total immersion in an activity in one or more imaginative feeling areas of experience."[12]

Key Idea: Hypnosis involves deep engagement and imagination.

William James

"Human beings can alter their lives by altering the attitudes of their minds."[13]

Key Idea: Mind-set changes can have significant life impacts.

Closing Thoughts

This chapter explored various perspectives on hypnosis, emphasising its diverse and complex nature. Understanding these viewpoints provides a richer insight into the psychological and therapeutic dimensions of hypnosis.

---

[11] https://en.wikipedia.org/wiki/George_Estabrooks
[12] https://en.wikipedia.org/wiki/Josephine_R._Hilgard
[13] https://en.wikiquote.org/wiki/William_James

Module 2: History of Hypnosis

In this exciting journey, we're going to delve into the fascinating world of hypnosis, exploring its origins, development, and various perspectives from eminent figures in the field.

Hypnosis, a state of heightened awareness and receptivity to ideas, has been a subject of intrigue and study by many. Notable figures like Milton Erickson, who described hypnosis as a state of focused attention, Martin T. Horn, Josephine Hilliard, and others, have contributed significantly to our understanding. Erickson, in particular, emphasised the importance of the hypnotic state in enabling clients to pay close attention to critical ideas.

We'll explore different definitions and views on hypnosis. William James, for instance, spoke about altering life by altering attitudes of the mind, while George H. Estabrooks highlighted its aspect of exaggerated suggestibility. Dave Elman, another key figure, defined hypnosis as a state where the critical faculty of the human mind is bypassed, allowing for selective thinking.

Throughout this module, we'll also trace the historical roots of hypnosis, dating back to ancient civilizations like the Babylonians, Greeks, and Egyptians.

The term 'hypnosis' derives from the Greek word 'Hypno,' meaning sleep, though the state of hypnosis is distinctly different from sleep. We'll discover how hypnosis has been a part of various cultures, including the Druids, Vikings, and various religious and spiritual practices.

We will also discuss the significant contributors to the field of hypnosis through different timelines. From Franz Anton Mesmer, who was pivotal in the 18th century, to more contemporary figures like Sigmund Freud and Emil Coué, each has left an indelible mark on the practice of hypnosis.

As we progress, we'll look at these historical figures and their contributions in more detail, understanding how their work has shaped modern hypnotherapy. This journey will not only provide historical context but also offer insights into the diverse techniques and philosophies that have shaped the art and science of hypnosis.

So, let's begin this fascinating exploration into the history of hypnosis, learning from the past to enhance our understanding and practice in the present.

Indeed, the pioneers of hypnosis, whom I've mentioned, have played a pivotal role in evolving and shaping the field. Their contributions have laid a foundation for modern practices, but as you rightly pointed out, the field of hypnosis shouldn't remain stagnant. It's essential to advance and expand upon these foundational teachings to explore new possibilities and enhance the practice.

Franz Anton Mesmer, born in 1734 and passing away in 1815, is a key figure in the history of hypnosis. Mesmer didn't actually practise hypnosis as we understand it today. Instead, he developed the concept of 'animal magnetism.'

This theory posited that a natural energetic transference occurred between all animated and inanimate objects. Mesmer believed that he could heal by channelling this 'magnetic' force.

Interestingly, Mesmer never used what we now call hypnotism. His focus was more on what he perceived as a supernatural magnetic force that could induce healing. His patients often experienced what was termed a 'crisis' during these sessions, which was thought to be a release or realignment of this magnetic force within the body.

Mesmer's practices and theories, while not directly hypnosis, were foundational in the evolution of the field. His concept of animal magnetism and the idea of influencing the mind or body through external means laid the groundwork for later developments in hypnotism.

Over time, Mesmer's followers adapted and modified his theories, gradually transitioning towards practices more recognizable as hypnotherapy today.

The evolution of hypnosis from Mesmer's animal magnetism to modern hypnotherapy underscores the importance of innovation and development in the field. As we delve deeper into this module, we'll explore how these early theories were transformed and how contemporary hypnotherapy has expanded upon them.

This will not only provide historical context but also inspire you to develop your own unique approach to hypnotherapy, pushing the boundaries of what's currently known and practised.

Here we are, exploring the rich history of hypnosis and its pioneers. Mesmer, known for his theories on healing through 'animal magnetism', laid the early foundations, though he didn't practise hypnosis as we understand it today. Mesmer's work, focusing on a supposed magnetic force for healing, set the stage for future developments in the field.

Moving forward, let's discuss *Count Maximilian de Puységur*, a notable figure born in 1784. As a student of Mesmer, Puységur discovered 'somnambulism' quite by accident. This discovery was pivotal, as it demonstrated the potential of the human mind to respond to suggestion even in a trance-like state.

He found that simple commands could influence the actions of a person in this state, leading to the concept of symbolism and the theta state - a state between being asleep and awake. This was crucial in understanding how words and symbols can be used in hypnosis.

James Braid, born in 1795, played a significant role in the evolution of hypnosis. He was a critic of mesmerism, which he saw as pseudoscientific. Braid modified mesmerist techniques and coined the term 'hypnotism'.

His approach focused on concentrated attention and suggestion, moving away from the concept of a mysterious force like Mesmer's magnetism. Braid is often considered a pioneer of modern hypnotism. Interestingly, he later attempted to rename hypnosis to 'mono idealism', emphasising the power of focusing attention on a single thought or idea.

James Esdaile, another key figure, was a British surgeon working in India around 1808-1859. He performed numerous surgeries using what became known as the Esdaile state or coma state, demonstrating the effectiveness of hypnosis in pain management, especially remarkable considering the lack of anaesthesia at that time.

Sigmund Freud, well-known for his contributions to psychoanalysis, also dabbled in hypnosis before developing his famous techniques of free association and psychoanalysis.

Emile Coué, a Frenchman who lived from 1857 to 1926, introduced the concept of auto-suggestion. His famous phrase, "Day by day, in every way, I'm getting better and better," illustrates the power of positive thinking and habitual reinforcement.

Lastly, *Milton H. Erickson*, a master of indirect and conversational hypnosis, demonstrated the ability to induce trance states without overtly mentioning hypnosis, showcasing the subtlety and depth of the practice.

As we delve into the history and contributions of these pioneers, remember that the field of hypnosis is ever-evolving. Their discoveries and methods lay a foundation for us to build upon, encouraging us to expand our understanding and develop new techniques that can aid in healing and personal development.

That concludes our exploration of hypnosis history in module two.

Next, we'll delve into module three, which focuses on the theory of the mind. I hope you're finding this journey as fascinating as I do, especially if it's a subject you're passionate about. It's my aim to guide you towards being the best you can be.

I'll be wrapping up this session shortly, but before I do, let's briefly touch upon what awaits in module three. It promises to be an enlightening continuation of our learning adventure. So, let's eagerly move forward and explore the intriguing theory of the mind together."

Chapter Summary: Understanding Hypnosis

As we wrap up module 2 of this course, let's revisit the key lessons in a straightforward and concise manner.

In this chapter, we delved into the fascinating history of hypnosis, exploring its evolution from the early concepts of animal magnetism to the sophisticated psychological practice it is today. We examined the contributions of key figures who were instrumental in shaping the understanding and methodologies of hypnosis.

Franz Anton Mesmer and his theory of animal magnetism laid the groundwork, despite his practices differing significantly from modern hypnotherapy.

Count Maximilian de Puységur, a student of Mesmer, accidentally discovered somnambulism, contributing significantly to the development of symbolic and suggestive aspects of hypnosis.

James Braid, a critic of mesmerism, redirected the focus to a more scientific approach, coining the term 'hypnotism'. He emphasised concentrated attention and suggestion rather than mystical forces.

James Esdaile demonstrated the practical applications of hypnosis in pain management in surgeries, showcasing its potential in medical settings.

Sigmund Freud briefly explored hypnosis before developing psychoanalysis, highlighting the transitional nature of psychological practices.

Emile Coué introduced the concept of auto-suggestion, emphasising the power of repetitive, positive self-affirmation.

Milton H. Erickson revolutionised hypnosis with his indirect and conversational techniques, proving its versatility and subtlety.

Closing Thoughts

"The future of hypnosis is in the hands of those who dare to explore."

- G. E. Loveday.

As we conclude this chapter, it's important to recognise that the field of hypnosis is dynamic and continually evolving. The pioneers we discussed laid the foundation, but the future of hypnosis is in the hands of those who dare to explore, innovate, and expand upon existing knowledge. The history of hypnosis is not just a record of the past but a stepping stone to future discoveries and advancements.

As students of this fascinating field, we're encouraged to think critically, experiment, and contribute to the ever-growing body of knowledge in hypnotherapy. Remember, the potential of hypnosis is limited only by our understanding and creativity. Let's carry forward the legacy of these pioneers with a passion for discovery and a commitment to helping others through the power of hypnosis.

Module 3: Hypnosis Timeline

1. Franz Anton Mesmer 1734 - 1815
2. Count Maxime de 1751–1825
3. James Braid 1795 – 1860
4. James Esdaile 1808 – 1859
5. Sigmund Freud 1856 – 19
6. Emile Coue 1857 – 1926
7. Milton H. Erickson 1901 – 1980
8. Geoffrey E Loveday 1953 – Present

Franz Anton Mesmer
(1734 - 1815)

Mesmer drew upon theories regarding healing by magnetism, going back to Paracelsus, to develop his concept of "animal magnetism", the main precursor of hypnotism.

However, Mesmer himself never hypnotised anyone but believed he "healed" by channelling a kind of supernatural "magnetism" into his patients' bodies which seemed capable of inducing an "emotional crisis." His theory and practices were adopted and modified by many followers.[14]

Count Maxime de Puységur
(1751–1825)

Maxime de Puységur,[15] a student of Mesmer, inadvertently discovered somnambulism. Similar to Mesmer, he utilised a so-called magnetic tree for his experiments. On one occasion, Puységur observed a young boy who had bound himself to this tree.

To Puységur's astonishment, the boy entered a sleep-like state with closed eyes. The Marquis, initially

[14] https://en.wikipedia.org/wiki/Franz_Mesmer
[15] https://en.wikipedia.org/wiki/Amand-Marie-Jacques_de_Chastenet,_Marquis_of_Puységur

alarmed, instructed the boy to release his knots. Remarkably, the boy compiled while remaining asleep. Puységur's further experiments included commanding the boy to walk and stop, which the boy executed flawlessly, even obeying the command to awaken.

This incident led Puységur to identify the phenomenon as somnambulism, thus establishing the term's association with hypnosis.

James Braid
(1795 – 1860)

Braid[16] was a passionate critic of Mesmerism which he saw as a pseudoscientific and supernatural theory.

He modified the techniques of the Mesmerists and coined the terms "hypnosis" and "hypnotic therapeutics" to describe his approach, which worked through focused attention and suggestion rather than postulating any mysterious force such as animal magnetism.

Braid is therefore normally considered to be the pioneer of hypnotism as opposed to Mesmerism. He introduced the term 'hypnosis'.[17]

---

[16] https://en.wikipedia.org/wiki/James_Braid_(surgeon)
[17] https://www.ukhypnosis.com/2019/07/25/beginners-guide-to-the-history-of-hypnosis-timeline/

James Esdaile
(1808 – 1859)

A Scottish surgeon in India, James Esdaile[18] performed 2000 operations, even amputations – with patients under hypno-anesthesia, which is feeling no pain.

Émile Coué
(1857 – 1926)

---

[18] https://en.wikipedia.org/wiki/James_Esdaile

Another Frenchman, Emile Coue, pioneered the use of autosuggestion6 and affirmations, for example:

'Day by day in every way, I am getting better and better.'

Sigmund Freud
(1856 – 1939)

Sigmund Freud, father of the cathartic method, free association and psychoanalysis, became interested in hypnosis and began to practise it. Not being very good at it, he went on to develop psychoanalysis instead.[19]

Milton H.Erickson
(1901-1980)

Milton H.Erickson, the recognised leading authority on clinical hypnosis, a master of indirect hypnosis, was able to put a person into a trance without even mentioning, the word hypnosis.[20]

---

[19] https://en.wikipedia.org/wiki/Sigmund_Freud
[20] https://en.wikipedia.org/wiki/Milton_H._Erickson

Geoffrey E. Loveday
(1953 – Present)

Author of five books. A Full-time professional hypnotherapist and a practitioner in pure-hypnoanalysis, complemented by his role as a Certified Hypnosis Instructor.

Beyond these roles, Loveday is the creator of Inherited Therapy and The Loveday Method, innovative approaches designed to heal and transform lives.[21]

The Loveday Method can be understood as a pioneering approach that uses advanced strategies to

---

[21] https://www.inheritedtherapy.com

delve into the layers of consciousness and embark on a retrospective journey.

This technique allows for the unlocking of dormant memories that are encoded in an individual's DNA, often serving as the root of inherited trauma.

The primary goal of this cutting-edge therapy is to tackle and heal longstanding traumas that are embedded in family histories, thereby unravelling the complex patterns that are interwoven into our genetic and conscious fabric.

Closing Thoughts

In conclusion, the Module 4 timeline of hypnosis pioneers from your course offers a comprehensive overview of the key figures and developments in the field of hypnosis and hypnotherapy. Starting with Franz Anton Mesmer in the 18th century and moving through to Geoffrey E Loveday in more recent times, this timeline encapsulates the evolution of hypnosis from a misunderstood phenomenon to a scientifically recognised and applied therapeutic technique. Each figure brought unique contributions:

- Mesmer introduced the concept of animal magnetism, setting the stage for future understanding of hypnotic states.

- De Puységur identified and described somnambulism, deepening the understanding of hypnotic trances.

- Braid formalised hypnosis as a psychological practice and coined the term itself.

- Esdaile demonstrated the practical application of hypnosis in pain management during surgery.

- Freud, though he eventually moved away from hypnosis, contributed to the exploration of the unconscious mind.

- Coue emphasised the power of autosuggestion, a principle still central in many hypnotherapy practices.

- Erickson revolutionised the field with his indirect approach and therapeutic use of storytelling and metaphors.

- Loveday represents the ongoing development and application of hypnotherapy in modern contexts using The Loveday Method.

Collectively, these pioneers have shaped the field of hypnotherapy, making it a versatile tool in psychology and medicine.

Their legacies continue to influence contemporary therapeutic practices, highlighting the ongoing relevance and importance of hypnosis in various aspects of mental health and wellbeing.

Module 4: The Theory of the Mind

Understanding the Structure of the Mind

12% of the conscious mind is dedicated to logic, decision-making, and analytical thinking.

88% of the subconscious mind is used, and part of that percentage of the subconscious mind holds memory from conception in this life. A significant portion of the subconscious mind is dedicated to storing memories, dating back to the very beginning of one's life.

The Critical Factor lays dormant between the conscious and the subconscious. Positioned between the conscious and subconscious realms, the critical factor remains inactive. It serves as a safeguard, functioning also as a selective filter between the two.

The Primitive mind is innate to every individual, and governs our instinctual responses, notably the fight-or-flight mechanism. Everyone is born with this basic instinct.

Key Points to Note:

Absence of the Critical Factor in Early Childhood: notably, the critical factor does not exist in children up to the age of 7.

The Learning Process: learning occurs through a three-step process:

A. Identification
B. Association
C. Response

Closing Thoughts

To summarise, the mind is a complex structure composed of different parts. The conscious mind focuses on logical thinking and decision-making, while the vast subconscious holds memories from the earliest stages of life.

The critical factor acts as a filter between these two parts but is notably absent in children under 7 years old. Learning in this framework involves identification, association, and responding to stimuli.

Module 5; Brain Wave States

Module 5 focuses on the theory of the mind, emphasising the importance of comprehending mental processes. This understanding is key to addressing various issues people face.

Let's dive in. I aim to simplify hypnosis, as I firmly believe in its ease and effectiveness as a tool for aiding others. Ready to begin?

We'll explore the conscious mind, known for its logic, and the subconscious mind, which acts like a computer, storing long-term memories, emotions, and habits. There's a barrier, often called the critical faculty, separating these two. The unconscious mind, meanwhile, manages automatic bodily functions like heartbeats and immune responses, things we don't consciously control.

Our focus will be on how the conscious mind, with its short-term memory and analytical abilities, interacts with the subconscious mind, a reservoir of emotions, creativity, intuition, and long-term memories. This interaction is key in understanding ourselves and in implementing hypnosis effectively.

We'll also discuss the theory that what you create within manifests externally. This means that our inner thoughts and feelings significantly influence our external experiences. Hypnosis taps into this by accessing the subconscious mind to effect change.

Further, we'll examine brainwave states, which range from the alert Beta state to the deep sleep Delta state. Understanding these states is essential for grasping how hypnosis works.

Throughout this module, I'll keep explaining these concepts in a simple, understandable way. Our journey through the mind promises to be enlightening and transformative. Let's move forward with curiosity and an open mind.

In this segment, we explore the different states of brain activity, particularly focusing on how these states can enhance activities like taking exams, playing sports, delivering presentations, and performing tasks requiring high concentration. The Theta level is associated with these activities, representing a basal level of normal waking state when our eyes are open.

Moving on to the Alpha state, this is where relaxation, visualisation, and creativity come into play. When we generate Alpha waves, we resonate with the Earth's frequency, often referred to as the 'Schumann Resonance'. This state is akin to what animals experience, hence the reference to the 'animal state'. It's a state of heightened intuition and awareness, often noticed in animals like dogs who perceive things beyond our normal senses.

In the Alpha state, with eyes closed, we experience passivity, relaxation, and a release from worries, fears, and frustrations. This state enhances intuition, inspiration, creativity, and expands our awareness beyond the usual limits of time and space. It is particularly effective for stress relief and is often used in hypnotic treatments.

There's a common belief among hypnotists that a light trance is sufficient for therapeutic purposes. However, I believe that a deeper state is necessary, as a light trance often leaves the conscious mind too active, potentially hindering the resolution of deeper issues. Patients might even doubt they were hypnotised due to the conscious mind's interference.

The Alpha state, while deeply relaxing, is not quite meditation. It allows us to access the wealth of creativity and knowledge that lies just below our conscious awareness, serving as a gateway to deeper states of consciousness. This state is crucial for delving into the subconscious and unlocking its potential, making it an integral part of our exploration into the mind and its capabilities. Let's proceed to the next part of our journey.

Theta level, the liminal state between wakefulness and sleep, is where we can access crucial subconscious information. Unlike scripted hypnotism, which might work for some but not all, working in the moment with empathy is more personal and effective. Theta involves waking dreams, daydreaming, and vivid imagination, allowing us to access information beyond our normal consciousness. It's a state where the mind expands beyond physical boundaries.

In Theta, repressed emotions and memories, often blocked during painful experiences for survival are stored. These repressions can manifest later as different symptoms. Theta is also where we can deeply influence the subconscious. Most people fall asleep in this state, but it's ideal for controlling heart rate, digestion, and entering deep meditation. It's the threshold where we can access and influence the subconscious mind.

For the next 21 days, each morning, close your eyes and visualise what you desire. Whether it's health, happiness, or personal goals, this practice can transform your aspirations into reality. The past is a lesson, the present a gift, and the future a new beginning.

Delta, the deepest sleep state, is where healing and body repair occur. Effective mind control in this state can lead to health rather than disease. Meditation in this state can enhance healing, control blood pressure, improve memory, and maximise intuition. Those with more Delta activity might even read minds better, like a 'first gear' of brain activity.

Brainwaves like all waves are measured in two ways. - frequency or speed of electrical pulses. Measured in cycles per second (cps) ranging from 0.5cps to 38cps.

Beta (14 – 21 CPS)

In the Beta frequency range (14-21 CPS), our minds are attuned to our physical senses: Vision, Hearing, Touch, Smell, and Taste. During this state, beta waves are predominant in our waking consciousness, focusing on cognitive tasks and external stimuli.

Beta is a state of 'rapid' mental activity characterised by: Alertness; Anxiety; Problem-solving; Judgement; Decision-making; Information processing; Mental engagement; and Focused concentration.

Programs centred on Beta frequencies are beneficial for tasks requiring heightened attention and mental acuity, such as: Preparing for an exam; Engaging in sports; Delivering a presentation; Analysing and organising data; and Performing activities that demand intense concentration.

In this context, Beta can be likened to a mental "fourth gear."

Alpha (7 – 14 CPS)

When we produce alpha waves, aligning with Earth's natural frequency, often referred to as the "Animal State," we experience a heightened sense of well-being, rejuvenation, and harmony.

This state is characterised by: A sense of passive tranquillity; Deep relaxation; Absence of worries, fears, or frustrations; Enhanced intuition; Burgeoning inspiration; Flourishing creativity; Connection with inner consciousness ;Perception of boundless time and space; Growing awareness; and Enriched learning.

Alpha wave generation is frequently advised for stress management. It represents a zone of profound relaxation that borders on, but is not quite, meditation. Here, we start tapping into the vast creative potential residing just beneath the surface of our conscious mind.

Alpha serves as a portal or entryway into a deeper level of consciousness. In essence, alpha is akin to a mental "third gear."

Theta (4 – 7 CPS)

In the Theta frequency range (4 – 7 CPS), associated with meditation, intuition, and memory, our state is akin to a waking dream or daydreaming.

This state is characterised by vivid mental imagery and openness to information beyond our usual conscious perception. Theta can induce deep meditative states, often accompanied by a sensation of 'floating,' and may create a feeling of your mind expanding beyond your physical body.

In Theta, our minds sometimes harbour hidden memories or secrets, particularly those we've suppressed during painful experiences as a means of emotional survival.

In this state, people often:
- Drift into sleep
- Gain control over physiological processes like heartbeat, bleeding, and digestion
- Engage in deep meditation, where brain activity slows to near-sleep levels

The Theta state is ideal for:

- Enhanced learning ('Super Learning')
- Mind reprogramming
- Improving dream recall
- Practising self-hypnosis
- Boosting mental activity
- Stress reduction
- Retrieving long-forgotten memories

Delta (0.5 – 4 CPS)

Delta waves, ranging from 0.5 to 4 CPS, are predominant in states of deep sleep, coma, or unconsciousness.

During these periods, the body undergoes significant repair and healing. Harnessing effective and constructive control of the mind in this state can lead to improved psychosomatic health, leveraging our inner mental levels to enhance intuitive abilities and streamline problem-solving by reducing reliance on guesswork.

Meditation practices enable individuals to traverse through various brainwave frequencies, including Delta.

Research indicates that engaging with these slower brain rhythms can significantly enhance various aspects of health and mental capacity.

Benefits observed include: Accelerated healing, often at rates much faster than normal; Improved regulation of blood pressure, muscle tension, and digestion; Enhanced productivity; Increased utilisation of intuitive abilities; Greater peace of mind; Improved learning and memory recall; and Maximisation of intuition.

It is also suggested that individuals with a higher delta activity may possess an enhanced ability to understand others' thoughts or intentions.

Delta waves represent the body's foundational 'first gear.'

As we conclude this course module, let's recap the essential teachings in a clear and concise manner.

As we wrap up the final module of this course, let's revisit the key lessons in a straightforward and concise manner:

Understanding the Mind: We started by exploring the Theory of Mind, learning about the conscious, subconscious, and unconscious minds. The conscious mind handles logical thinking and short-term memory, the subconscious stores emotions, habits, and long-term memories, and the unconscious manages automatic bodily functions.

Hypnosis Demystified: Hypnosis was introduced as a simple yet effective tool for personal development and therapy. We learned how it can be used to access and influence the subconscious mind.

Interplay of Mind States: We delved into how our inner thoughts and feelings shape our external experiences. Understanding this concept is crucial for personal growth and for effectively using hypnosis.

Brainwave States: The course covered different brainwave states – Beta (alertness), Alpha (relaxation and creativity), Theta (subconscious access), and Delta (deep sleep and healing). Each state has its unique significance in understanding our mental processes.

Practical Application: We emphasised practical techniques, such as the 21-day visualisation practice, to apply our learning in real life. This exercise helps in transforming thoughts into reality.

Power of Visualisation: The importance of visualising goals and desires was highlighted as a powerful tool for personal transformation.

Deeper Understanding of Self: The course aimed to provide tools for a deeper understanding of oneself and how to harness the power of the mind for better well-being and fulfilment.

Continuous Learning: Finally, we acknowledged that learning about the mind is an ongoing process. We encouraged continued exploration and application of these concepts in everyday life.

As we close this module, remember that the journey through the mind is continuous, and the insights gained are tools for lifelong learning and growth. Keep exploring, applying, and transforming with an open mind and heart.

Closing Thoughts

As we conclude this module, it's important to reflect on the profound journey through the intricacies of the human mind. We've explored the delicate interplay between the conscious, subconscious, and unconscious mind, gaining insights into how these layers shape our perceptions, behaviours, and overall well-being.

The exploration of hypnosis and its application as a tool for personal growth and healing stands out as a significant aspect of this journey. By demystifying hypnosis, we've opened doors to a world where mental processes can be navigated and influenced for positive change.

The discussion around the manifestation of internal thoughts into external realities underscores the power of the mind. It highlights how our inner world significantly impacts our external experiences, and how, by understanding and harnessing this power, we can effect profound changes in our lives.

The exploration of brainwave states - Beta, Alpha, Theta, and Delta - provides a scientific grounding to our understanding of the mind's functioning. Each state offers unique insights into our mental capacities and potential for growth and healing.

The emphasis on practical applications, such as the 21-day visualisation practice, not only provides tools for personal development but also empowers us to take active steps towards realising our goals and aspirations.

As we close this chapter, it's crucial to recognize that the journey through the mind is ongoing. The insights and knowledge gained are not just for temporary contemplation but for lifelong application. The mind is a vast and dynamic landscape, constantly evolving and responding to our experiences and actions.

Let's move forward with a renewed sense of curiosity, openness, and a commitment to exploring the depths of our minds. May this journey bring about transformative changes, leading to a deeper understanding of ourselves and a more fulfilled, conscious life.

In our next session, we will discuss the importance of a passionate connection with clients and the power of belief in the hypnotic process. The mind's power is immense, and with the right approach, anything is possible. Let's reconvene in Module 6 for further exploration. See you then, and have a great day!

Module 6: Belief in Yourself

Hello, everyone! I'm excited to announce that we're adding an additional module to our series, focusing on a crucial topic: belief in yourself. This module is designed to deepen our understanding of the power of self-belief and its critical role in both personal and professional growth.

It's not just about acquiring new skills or knowledge, but also about nurturing a strong, positive belief in your own abilities. This belief is the foundation upon which we build success and overcome challenges. Stay tuned for more insights and transformative strategies in this upcoming module.

This belief in yourself is indeed vital. Many of you might question your abilities, wondering, "Can I really do this? Can I successfully hypnotise someone?" These doubts are natural, but they also signify stepping out of your comfort zone, which is a crucial part of growth and learning.

Embracing this discomfort is key to developing confidence in your skills and capabilities. This upcoming module will focus on fostering this self-belief, guiding you to overcome self-doubt and embrace the challenges that lead to personal and professional development.

Embracing this discomfort and challenging yourself is the key to building confidence and enhancing your skills. It's about transforming the question "Can I do this?" into the affirmation "I can and I will do this." This mind-set shift is what this module aims to cultivate.

Remember, your belief in yourself is a powerful tool, not just in hypnosis. By fostering this self-belief, you'll not only improve your hypnotic abilities but also empower yourself to make meaningful changes in your life and the lives of others.

That's right, I'm currently discussing the importance of self-belief, especially when it comes to the art of hypnosis. You must start by believing in yourself. Belief is powerful; with it, you can accomplish almost anything.

Hypnosis is a remarkable tool and can profoundly impact people's lives, but the key is to have faith in your abilities. If you don't believe in yourself, it's unlikely others will believe in you.

Now, let's talk about what happens when you hypnotise someone for the first time. It's common to feel a mix of exhilaration and doubt after bringing someone out of a trance. You might wonder, "Did it really work? What did they experience?" However, as a professional, you can't let these doubts show. It's crucial to maintain confidence and assurance in your skills.

Believing in what I'm teaching is essential. You must trust that your subjects will enter a trance and that you can assist them effectively. It's not just about inducing trance; it's about understanding the various stages of the process: inducing the trance, working with the subject during the trance, and then bringing them out of it.

As we wrap up the final module of this course, let's revisit the key lessons in a straightforward and concise manner.

Welcome to the summary of Module 6, which focuses on a pivotal theme in our series: the power of self-belief.

This module is not just about learning new skills or knowledge, but fundamentally about nurturing a robust and positive belief in your own capabilities.

Here are the key takeaways:

Importance of Self-Belief: We emphasised the critical role self-belief plays in both personal and professional growth. Belief in oneself is the foundation for success and overcoming challenges.

Overcoming Self-Doubt: Many might question their abilities, especially in contexts like learning hypnosis. We discussed how these doubts, while natural, are indicators of stepping out of your comfort zone, an essential step for growth and learning.

Embracing Discomfort: Embracing discomfort is essential for building confidence. This module encourages transforming doubts from "Can I do this?" to a confident "I can and I will do this."

Mind-set Shift: The module aims to cultivate a mind-set shift, reinforcing that belief in oneself is a powerful tool, not just in hypnosis but in all aspects of life. By fostering self-belief, you empower yourself to effect meaningful changes in your life and in the lives of others.

Professional Confidence: We discussed the experience of hypnotising someone for the first time, acknowledging the mix of exhilaration and doubt that may follow. The module stressed the importance of maintaining professional confidence and assurance in your skills.

Trust in the Process: It's crucial to trust in the hypnotic process, understanding the stages of inducing trance, working with the subject during the trance, and bringing them out of it.

This module, therefore, serves as a cornerstone in building a strong, unwavering belief in your abilities, which is essential not only for mastering hypnosis but also for navigating various aspects of life. As we move to the next module, remember to carry this sense of self-confidence and belief in your journey ahead.

Closing Thoughts

As we close Module 6, "Belief in Yourself," it's vital to reflect on the profound insights and transformative strategies we've explored. This module wasn't just about acquiring new skills or knowledge in hypnosis; it was fundamentally about nurturing a strong, positive belief in your own abilities.

In closing, remember that the journey of self-belief is ongoing and dynamic. Each step forward, each challenge faced, and each doubt overcome adds to your reservoir of confidence and capability. Carry these insights forward as you continue on your path of personal and professional development.

Module 7: The Esdaile State – Hypnotic Coma

James Esdaile

This doesn't happen every time, but there is a possibility that someone may not come out of hypnosis when you count them out. This is RARE, but it can happen.

The reason for this is that the trance is so amazing, that they don't want to wake up.

What to do:

1. Don't panic

2. With time, they will naturally come out of that state

3. More authoritative (suggestion to alertness)

4. Count them up from 1 – 5

5. DANGER

6. Elman Technique: 'in a moment, I'm going to count to 3 and if you do not wake, you will never be put in this relaxed state again.'

7. Engage intellect with normal conversation

Closing Thoughts

It's important to address the concern about someone not coming out of hypnosis, which is a topic that occasionally comes up in discussions about hypnotic practice.

Here's a breakdown of your points and some additional context:

Don't Panic: This is crucial. Hypnosis is a state of focused attention and relaxation, not unconsciousness. It's rare for someone to not "wake up" from hypnosis, but maintaining calm is key to handling the situation effectively.

Natural Emergence: Most individuals will naturally exit the hypnotic state over time. The trance state is not unlike daydreaming or being deeply engrossed in a book or movie; people eventually shift out of it.

More Authoritative Suggestions: Sometimes a firmer, more authoritative tone or instruction can help guide the person back to full alertness.

Counting Technique: This is a standard technique where the hypnotist counts, usually from 1 to 5, with each number representing increasing alertness. It's a simple and effective way to signal the end of the session.

DANGER: Shift the person's mind out of the hypnotic state and back to regular waking consciousness. This may involve using a clear, firm command or employing a sudden change in tone or physical stimulus (like clapping hands) to prompt an immediate return to full alertness.

Elman Technique: Named after Dave Elman, a noted hypnotist, this technique involves a kind of ultimatum where the subject is told they will lose the ability to enter this relaxed state if they don't wake up. This can be effective because it creates a sense of loss.

Engage Intellect: Initiating normal conversation can help shift the person's mind out of the hypnotic state and back to regular waking consciousness.

It's important to note that while the idea of someone not coming out of hypnosis can be concerning, it's extremely rare and often more related to the individual not wanting to leave a state of relaxation, rather than being unable to do so.

Professional training in hypnosis includes learning how to handle such situations effectively and ethically. If you are practising hypnosis, it is crucial to have proper training and to understand the ethical considerations involved in working with individuals in a hypnotic state.

Module 8: Abreaction

Abreaction is a psychoanalytical concept, originally developed by Sigmund Freud. It refers to the process of releasing repressed emotions by reliving a past traumatic experience. The idea is that by confronting and expressing these emotions, a person can alleviate psychological distress.[22]

The concept of abreaction was particularly prominent in early psychoanalysis and trauma therapy. It was thought that bringing the unconscious memories of a traumatic event to conscious awareness, often accompanied by an emotional outburst, would lead to catharsis and therapeutic relief.

However, it's important to note that the theories and practices around abreaction have evolved and been subject to criticism over time. Modern psychology and trauma treatment often incorporate more nuanced

---

[22] https://www.sciencedirect.com/topics/nursing-and-health-professions/abreaction#:~:text=Clinically%2C%20Freud%20initially%20worked%20using,%E2%80%93%20the%20%27cathartic%20method%27.

understandings of memory, emotion, and the therapeutic process.

Techniques that encourage the controlled expression of emotions and the careful processing of traumatic memories are more common, with an emphasis on the safety and stability of the patient.

Example

- Emotional
- Crying
- Screaming
- Hitting out
- Shaking

What to do

- Stay Calm
- Do not touch
- Scene Fades
- Feel chair and know you're safe
- Bring them out

Closing Thoughts

In summary, abreaction, in simple terms, would be like summarising the key points about it. Abreaction is like going back to a really upsetting memory and feeling all those strong emotions again, but this time in a safe place where you can understand and deal with them better.

It's based on the idea that if you face these old, hidden feelings, you can feel better and less troubled by them in your everyday life.

However, how we understand and use abreaction has changed a lot, and nowadays, therapists are more careful about how they help people deal with tough memories.

They focus more on making sure the person feels safe and stable, rather than just reliving the past emotions.

Module 9: H+ Intent

"A profound passion and an unbreakable bond between you and the client, marked by an intense, burning desire to hypnotise someone, where the allure of the hypnotic process creates a deep and meaningful connection."

In cultivating a deep-seated passion and fostering an undeniable connection with the client, you are driven by an overwhelming and fervent desire to delve into the realm of hypnosis.

This desire is not just a mere interest but a compelling need, a calling to engage in the hypnotic process. Your commitment to this art form is rooted in a profound understanding and respect for its power, forming a bond with your client that goes beyond the ordinary, creating a shared journey into the depths of the subconscious.

This intense yearning to hypnotise is fueled by a genuine intent to explore and understand the human mind, bridging gaps in consciousness and unlocking hidden potentials within.

Let's revisit the key lessons in a straightforward and concise manner.

In this context, it's important to recognise that effective hypnosis relies not just on the skill of the hypnotist, but also on the rapport they build with their client.

This relationship is based on trust, understanding, and a mutual commitment to the goals of the session. The hypnotist's passion and desire to hypnotise play a significant role in creating a conducive environment for the hypnotic process.

Moreover, your emphasis on the intense desire to hypnosis indicates a recognition of the power and responsibility that comes with the practice. It's a field that requires not only technical skill but also a deep understanding of human psychology and empathy.

Closing Thoughts

In conclusion, the art of hypnosis is deeply rooted in the connection and trust established between the hypnotist and the client. This relationship is enhanced by the hypnotist's passion and intense desire to explore the realms of the mind, underpinned by a strong ethical foundation and a respect for the client's experience.

Hypnosis transcends mere technique; it's a blend of psychology, empathy, and effective communication, offering profound insights into human consciousness. It's a field that demands continuous learning, understanding, and respect for the transformative power it holds.

Whether for therapeutic purposes or personal growth, the practice of hypnosis represents a unique intersection of science, art, and the depths of human interaction

Module 10: The Three Section Process

1. Pre-Talk Session: Learning essential questions to initiate the process.

2. Trance Induction: Understanding and applying techniques for entering a trance state.

3. The Ancestral Journey: Techniques to access specific brain regions for navigating the mind and reliving ancestral experiences.

When reading my book, 'The Loveday Method,' it's important to focus on three core elements:

The Pre-Talk: This is about understanding the client, establishing a connection, and setting the stage for effective hypnosis.

Deep Trance Induction: This crucial step involves guiding the client into a profound trance to reach the subconscious.

Addressing the Core Issue: Using the unique techniques of The Loveday Method, this phase involves working directly on the client's primary concern. The method includes navigating specific brain regions to relive and release ancestral experiences, particularly those issues that have been deeply ingrained since before birth.

Closing Thoughts

"In conclusion, the journey of hypnosis, as outlined in The Loveday Method, is a profound exploration of the mind, anchored in three pivotal phases:

The Pre-Talk: This initial stage is crucial in laying the foundation for the entire hypnotic process. Here, the hypnotist delves into understanding the client on a deeper level, establishing a strong and trusting connection. It's not just a conversation but a strategic preparation that sets the stage for a successful and effective hypnosis session.

Deep Trance Induction: This phase marks the heart of the journey. The hypnotist, with skill and precision, guides the client into a deep, profound trance. It's in this state, beyond the ordinary layers of consciousness, that the client can access the vast and untapped potential of their subconscious mind. This step is not just about depth but about reaching a transformative level of awareness.

Addressing the Core Issue: The final and perhaps the most crucial phase involves using the specialised techniques of The Loveday Method to directly address the client's primary concern. This method isn't just a tool; it's a gateway to exploring and navigating specific brain regions, allowing the client to relive and ultimately release ancestral experiences. These are not just any experiences, but deeply ingrained issues, often rooted in the client's psyche since before their birth.

Each phase is integral, and together, they form a comprehensive approach to healing and transformation.

The Loveday Method isn't just a methodology; it's a journey through time and consciousness, providing a path to resolving issues that transcend the individual, reaching back through the ancestral lineage."

Module 11.The Pre-talk – The Secret Formula

Before we teach you the Pre-talk, allow me to delve deeper into why the Pre-talk is not just unique, but remarkably effective.

Imagine a scenario where each client who approaches you is already filled with unwavering confidence in your abilities. They come to you, not with doubts, but with a firm belief that you hold the key to their well-being.

They are so convinced of your expertise that they are prepared to invest any amount necessary to achieve their desired health and wellness.

Yes, that's right; any amount. This might sound like a far-fetched dream, but it's a reality, one that has been proven time and again through the creative use of The Loveday method.

Now, think of this not just as a professional skill, but as possessing a magical ability to attract prosperity. It's similar to possessing a secret formula that turns your expertise into financial success.

Let me take you on a journey back to my own beginnings in this field. When I first started my career in hypnosis, I was as much a learner as a practitioner.

Yet, as I navigated through the intricacies of the human mind, I discovered patterns and techniques that not only helped my clients but also transformed my practice into a thriving venture.

It's a story of growth, learning, and the undeniable power of the mind, a story that I am eager to share with you.

The story begins

My story begins years ago, in a time of personal hardship. I lost my wife and was left to raise five children on my own. Imagine a life resembling 'The Holiday' movie - being both a mother and a father, managing everything single-handedly.

Raising children is challenging enough, but doing it with financial strain adds another layer. Picture this: 22

maxed-out credit cards £60,000 in debt. That's right — sixty thousand pounds, and a constant struggle to bring more money in.

Sleepless nights were the norm as I toiled for 60 to 70 hours a week, merely surviving. Have you ever felt that? I'm sure you have.

But then, I faced a crucial question: What could I do differently? Clients got in touch with me, but only 40 percent of those who contacted me wanted my help; and out of them, 10 percent never followed through. I needed to identify what was going wrong.

That's when I changed my approach. I developed a unique 'pre-talk'; a game-changer that drastically shifted the dynamics.

This wasn't just a change; it was a transformation. The results were astonishing - from 30 percent of clients saying 'yes' to an overwhelming 99 percent.

What I discovered and applied has not only changed my professional life but has the potential to revolutionise yours too.

Dive into my story, and you might just find the keys to unlocking your own success.

Understanding the Value of My Experience

As my journey progressed, I came to a significant realisation; my clients were not just seeking my help, they were prepared to invest substantially in the solutions I offered.

Initially, I charged £30 per session, with payments made after each meeting. However, this approach needed to change.

I recognised the true value of my services and understood that my pricing strategy had to change.

The willingness of clients to pay any amount for their well-being was a clear indicator that I was offering something invaluable. This insight was crucial, leading me to rethink and change my pricing system to reflect the real value of the help and change I was offering.

Taking a Big Risk

Picture this: I'm about to step out of my comfort zone, heart racing with nerves. Instead of just offering single sessions, I envision something bigger – a complete six-session program.

It's an exciting leap, not just for me but also for my clients, who would now receive a bonus free session as part of the package.

Just Imagine this – clients paying upfront for all six sessions. This means their commitment is locked in, and I have financial security, regardless of any missed appointments. It's a win-win.

Let's now discuss the substantial rise in price. From charging £30 for a single session, I'm considering £600 for the entire program.

It's a huge step, right? Money was trickling in, and I was just getting by, but I had bigger dreams for my children and me.

That night, after setting this new price, I couldn't sleep. My mind was racing with thoughts. In your opinion, do you believe that this could work? You know I had doubts too.

Step into my shoes at that moment, feeling the anticipation and the hope that this decision would mark the beginning of something great. You know, that feeling kept me going.

Transforming Lives, Including Mine

Imagine the day after I had bravely switched to a program approach. My phone was buzzing with clients responding to the pre-talk, each one eagerly saying 'yes' to the sessions.

But then came the moment of truth – discussing the new price. I gently reminded them that all prices were on my website, although, to my surprise, 80% hadn't even looked.

Now, picture the scene: I reveal the price - £600 for six sessions. What do you think they said? To my amazement they said YES.

Whether they knew the price beforehand or were hearing it for the first time, their reactions were the same – not a hint of shock, just a simple nod of agreement. It felt like a dream.

This was a turning point. Clients willingly paid the new fee, drastically changing not only their lives but mine as well. Today, in January 2024, the journey has led me to charge £799 or £899 for these life-altering six-session programs.

Single sessions are a thing of the past. Join me in this remarkable story of growth, challenge, and how important it is to believe in yourself.

Experience the Proof Yourself

Don't just take my word for it – see for yourself the truth in my story. I invite you to visit my website at www.liverpoolhypnosis.co.uk. There, you can check out the prices for yourself and see the evidence of my journey and success.

But there's more. As a special thank you for purchasing my book, I'm offering you an exclusive opportunity. I will personally teach you the secret formula of the pre-talk in a special group session.

And guess what? It's completely free. This session will be held on Zoom, making it accessible no matter where you are. I'm here to share this valuable knowledge with a group of 7 to 10 like-minded individuals.

All you need to do is visit my website, and complete a short questionnaire to reserve your place. This is my gift to you – a chance to learn a transformative technique at no cost, alongside peers who are just as eager to discover the power of the Secret Formula!

Don't miss this special chance to learn the secret pre-talk formula together with others in a fun and engaging way.

Secure your spot NOW:
https://www.inheritedtherapy.com/apply

Preparing the client

The therapist does not give the client a form to fill in; instead, they get to know them and make each session tailored for them.

The Pre-Talk builds rapport, trust, and belief with the client; they will know you can help them.

So here is my gift to you: The Pre-Talk.

Dig deep into their family history, and build rapport.

Ask them these basic questions:

- Age
- Date of birth
- Name
- Address
- Are they seeing a Doctor at the moment?
- Are they on any medication?
- Have they ever been on antidepressants?
- Do they have any heart problems?
- Have they ever been hypnotised?
- If so, why and what for?
- Are they asthmatic?
- Do they suffer from any recurring pain?
- If a woman, is she pregnant?
- Do they have Epilepsy?

(If they have epilepsy or heart problems, you may need a doctor's referral. Use your common sense.)

Ask them if they suffer from any of the following:

- Depression
- Anxiety
- Stress
- Sadness
- Loneliness
- Worry
- Anger
- Panic attacks
- Regret
- Guilt
- Blaming yourself
- Blaming others.
- Do they regularly get emotional?

Next, talk about all their relationships, from the very first to the latest.

- Are they married?
- Do they have a partner?
- Do they have children?
- If a woman, is she pregnant?
- Do they love them?
- Are they, or were they afraid of them?

Asking these questions is so important. And it should be asked whether the relationship was good or bad. Ask if there has been any violence in the home.

Have they ever been hit by their partner? Were they intimidated by them? If so/not, why did it end? Ask them how they felt about it all.

Then move on to a different question:

"If I had a magic wand, what would you want me to help you with?"

You will find the answer will be very different from the reasons why they came to you in the first place. Then ask them:

"If you had one wish, what would you ask for?"

Once you have this information, move on to the following questions. First, let's dig deeper with them and talk about their family, their mum and dad. But be gentle with how you word it. This would be my approach:

"I don't mean to upset you in any way, but I have to ask these questions to help me understand how I can best help you. Is that ok with you?"

Ask the questions about their family:

"Did you have a good childhood?"

If yes, go to the next question. If no, "was there violence in the home? Did you ever see your dad hit your mum? Or your mum hit your dad?"

"Are your parents alive?"

If no, ask further questions:

- How old were you when it happened?
- Do you miss them?
- Who were you brought up by, your mum's or your dad's parents?

If yes, ask further questions again:

- Do you love your mum?
- Do you love your dad?
- Who are you closest to, mum or dad?
- Do you have any brothers and sisters?
- Do you love them?

It's not just about asking the right questions; it's also about the answers that will take you closer to helping them.

And please, listen and watch their reaction to the answers they give; look into their eyes. You are looking for the answers to their problem concerning the people they have lost.

Further Questions:

"Is there anyone in your family that has passed away recently that you were close to?"

Now, this is where you have to ask questions in a certain way, by asking them three times after they have answered each time.

Example:

Patient: No, it was a long time ago.
Hypnotist: Think like a child?
Patient: I can't remember.

My three questions would be:

"When you were little, were you close to your mum, dad, grandfather, grandmother, aunt or uncle?"
"How old were you when they died?"

"How close were you?"

Next, ask them the following most essential questions:

- Is there a family member who died before they were born?
- On mum's side or dad's side?
- What did they die of?

This links to:

"Inherited Therapy and The Loveday Method."

In your following questions, talk about their school: Have they ever been bullied? If yes: what year was it, primary or high school, and for how long? Was it mental abuse or physical abuse?

The Trance

Now we explain hypnosis to the client. Get them to close their eyes and ask them questions:

What noises can you hear? If they can't hear anything, tap on the table. With their eyes closed, they may be aware of a flickering of the eyelids or a tingling in their fingers. Then get them to open their eyes.

Ask them if they think they were hypnotised. Some will say yes, and most will say no. Look them in the eyes and say:

"How do you know?"

They will think inwardly at that moment and answer, "I was aware." At that point, tell them they were not hypnotised...

In hypnosis, you are not unconscious, you are not asleep, and you are aware. Your awareness increases by up to two thousand per cent when in hypnosis.

These are the four stages of awareness:

Beta: When your eyes are open, you are in Beta, where the brain waves travel up to 21 cycles per second.

Alpha: When you close your eyes, you are in alpha; The brain waves travel up to 14 cycles per second.

Theta: This is the borderline between sleep and awake; brain waves travel up to seven cycles per second. This is where we need to take the client.

Delta: which is sleep brain waves travel up to four cycles per second.

Then you explain about Dave Elman, a fantastic hypnotist. He used to teach doctors, dentists, physicians, and surgeons to be able to take people into an operating room and perform operations without any anaesthetic.

He devised the "Pinpoint Method", where he could take you back to the first time you walked. Do you Remember the first time you walked? Or your first birthday, where you will see everything? When your Mum was healthy, and so were you. She held you for the very first time in her arms.

He could take you back into your mother's womb, where you would feel everything your mother was going through and what she was feeling. You are more connected than you think.

He believed that hypnosis is a state of mind where you could bypass the critical factor between conscious and subconscious, and selective thinking would be established.

For example, he would have a doctor sitting in the chair with all the doctors watching. He would say, "in a moment, not yet, in a moment".

Now, say this to the client:

"You will close your eyes, they will lock tight, but you will not be able to open them".

Repeat to the client: "Now close your eyes, lock them tight now, and try to separate them. You find you can't."

For a split second, they try but cannot open their eyes immediately. Say "stop trying", and tell them to open their eyes. At that moment, they will realise that you can help them.

Next, get them to close their eyes, imagine their right or left hand, and get them to nod their head once they have. Get them to picture or imagine a set of stairs again. Get them to nod their head. Ask, "do the stairs go up or down? What are they made of? Are the stairs old or new? Are they stairs you know or don't know? When you look at the stairs, what do you feel? What age are you?"

Now get them to picture or imagine a door. Ask what colour the door is. Is it panelled or flat? Old or new? Is it a door you know or one you don't know? What age are you when you are looking at the door? What do you feel when you look at the door?

When asking the questions, echo everything back to them. (Repeat their answers back to them.)

This Pre-Talk is unique.

Now ask them to close their eyes and get them to imagine their right or left hand. Get them to lift the wrist of their right or left arm and allow the fingertips to touch the arm of the chair or their thigh barely.

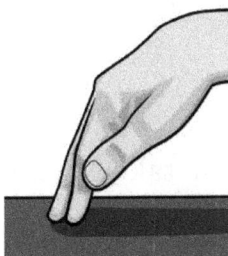

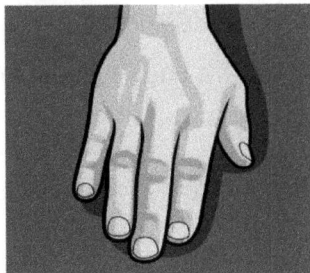

Then tell them: "Now, you will allow your wrist to raise, becoming lighter, as light as a feather."

By being persistent and repeating these words, the hand will become lighter; light as a feather, lifting, rising, pulling, tugging.

As soon as the hand rises, and it will rise, it will form a belief in the client's mind.

Now, what have you learned about the client?

1. They can follow instructions.
2. Their eyes were stuck, and they couldn't open their eyes.
3. They can visualise.
4. Their hand will rise.

Now you are given the tools to help them. I have mentioned this in a previous chapter, and I have to bring it up again because I feel it is imperative to know when to ask these questions.

These three questions have been taken from the book;

"It Didn't Start With You" by Mark Wolynn.[23]

The use of Inherited Therapy, The Loveday Method, Hypnotherapy, and Regression will take it to a whole new level.

So, I ask you these simple questions: Where do these negative, controlling emotions come from?

1. What negative thoughts go through your mind that you keep repeating to yourself day in and day out?
2. Did these feelings originate with you?
3. Think back to your family history; is there someone from your family who had the same issues you are experiencing now?

[23] Wolynn, M., 2017. It Didn't Start with You. Penguin Publishing Group, p.125.

Next, we give them an understanding of why they feel this way, that the feelings were not theirs in the first place. They were not to blame; it was not their fault. And the feelings that they are holding on to were there before they were born.

Now, by this time, you should know why they feel the way they do and how you can help them. You do this by drawing.

Firstly, you explain about the conscious and subconscious. "The subconscious judges, analyses, and rationalises, you are analysing me to see if I know what I'm talking about."

At that moment, they may smile as if you are reading their mind.

The conscious mind has a short memory. It can only remember small amounts of information: 7 plus 2, or 7 minus 2. This isn't completely true since everyone is different, and some people can remember more or less. There is a barrier between the conscious and subconscious called the Critical Factor, which allows information in and out. The subconscious is different. It holds 95 to 99 per cent of memory; it knows everything about you.

It is truly a miracle knowing the first time you walked, the first time you talked. It allows your blood to flow, your heart to work, it keeps you alive, and it gives the gifts of being able to use all your senses.

1. Hearing (Auditory)
2. Smell (Olfactory)
3. Taste (Gustatory)
4. Touch (Tactile)
5. Sight (Visual)
6. Vestibular (Movement awareness of one's body in space)

The vestibular system refers to the structures in the inner ear responsible for sensing motion and head position. The vestibular system has three main parts: the semi-circular canals, the utricle, and the saccule. Within these structures, hair cells sense movement from both angular acceleration (movement around a point, like spinning) and linear acceleration (like jumping).

When these hair cells are activated, they begin a transduction process that leads to the release of neurotransmitters, which stimulate afferent neurons. These afferent neurons help relay information from the vestibular system to the cerebellum and brainstem.

The primary function of this vestibular system is to help us maintain balance and posture. The more we know about the innervation of muscles activated by the vestibular system, the better we will be able to understand how body orientation and eye movements work together in relation to each other.

7. Proprioception (a new study suggests this may have a genetic basis, how your brain understands where your body is in space).[24]

More than just a "sense of balance," proprioception is the brain's ability to locate our body parts. For example, it helps you know where your hands are if they become invisible after you close your eyes.[25]

---

[24] Shadrach, J.L., Gomez-Frittelli, J. and Kaltschmidt, J.A. (2021).
[25] "Proprioception Revisited: Where do we Stand? Current Opinion in Physiology."

8. Interoception: It is the sense that alerts us to stimuli involving our internal organs. This is because each organ has specialised sensory neurons called "receptors" designed for this purpose.

These receptors, either chemoreceptors or mechanoreceptors, monitor things like temperature, pH status (acidosis vs alkalosis), oxygen concentration, and fluid levels in the blood, among other things.

For example, chemoreceptors monitor glucose secretions from the pancreas while mechanoreceptors monitor stretch within the veins' walls or detect certain chemicals in our stomachs.

Interoception also involves awareness of our heart rate. This is interesting because it is not associated with any of the traditional five senses. Moreover, Interoception has been found to have a significant role in self-awareness, emotional experience, and consciousness.

We are quite impressive.

So we relax the conscious mind and bypass the critical factor to stimulate the unconscious mind. We take the bad out and put in the good. Then, change the habits and beliefs of how you think and feel.

So, what does that mean? Imagine you had to write a speech. After finishing, place it down on the table, or if it's on the computer, save it. Then, you drink, realise part of it is wrong, go back to the speech you have written, delete the information you don't want, and put new information in.

Very much like the mind, we take it out and put new information in. That is the direction we need to go in, like suggestion therapy. The big question we need to ask ourselves is, why?

Why do I feel this way? I know you have been searching for the answers.

Cause and effect

For every cause, there is an effect, a reason why. So now look at the effect.

Now you go through the clients' notes and see what is affecting their life; depression, anxiety, stress, panic attacks, emotional sadness, fear, and anger; this is the effect it's having on them.

And if we knew why, it wouldn't be there.

An analogy would be if there were a leak in the ceiling, and I came along with paint and told you that painting the leak would cure the problem.

No it won't. And yet, physicians prescribe antidepressants without understanding why.

So, you hire a plumber who discovers a leaky pipe. "You have a leaky pipe, Mrs Jones." So you say: repair it. He then replaces the pipe, which results in no damp floor boards or carpet, allowing you to paint the room.

The problem is solved once we identify the root cause. Now, this is where it gets really interesting.

Now explain to them: The Loveday Method - Inherited Therapy

It's a common belief that when we're born, our life is like a blank slate, with no prior history or baggage. But, this is actually a misconception.

Think about it this way: it's hard to imagine that the lives of people who lived 100 or even 500 years ago could affect us today.

However, this influence is much closer and more real than you might think. Let's use a simple example: do you resemble your mother or father? You might share their physical features or even personality traits.

This similarity comes from your DNA, which is a blend of genetic material from your parents. But it doesn't stop there.

Your parents received their DNA from your grandparents, who got it from your great-grandparents, and so on.

This chain of genetic transfer doesn't just carry physical traits but can also include health conditions like cancer, diabetes, and heart disease, passed down through generations.

Now, if physical traits and health conditions can be inherited, it's also possible that emotional traits are passed down in a similar way, becoming part of our makeup even before we're born.

According to epigenetics, a field that studies how genes are influenced by external factors, it's possible that we carry genetic memories from our ancestors, potentially going back as far as 14 generations.

Explain by use of a story; Past Life or Inherited; You Decide.

Approximately five years ago, I had the opportunity to speak before a group of about fifty psychologists. During this event, I invited a woman to join me on stage for a demonstration of hypnosis. In the preliminary conversation, known as the Pre-Talk, she shared with the audience her deep-seated sadness, which visibly moved her.

She recounted the loss of her beloved puppy, which she cherished like her own child. The puppy's illness and subsequent passing deeply affected her. That same year, she also experienced the loss of her father, leaving her without any close family support.

Additionally, she mentioned an incident from when she was seventeen — a broken ankle that continued to cause her intense pain. She also described a persistent tightness in her chest, a discomfort she had felt since her early years, accompanied by severe and recurring headaches.

This was the beginning of a remarkable journey into her past. Through the hypnosis session, we guided her back in time, hundreds of years, to a life where she was a fifteen-year-old boy tasked with delivering an urgent message. In this past life, she was hiding in the woods, understanding that capture could mean execution.

In the hypnosis session, I guided her to a pivotal moment in her past life that was impacting her current life. In that lifetime, as a man, she was discovered in a dungeon, gravely injured, lying in a pool of blood. He had a severe head wound and an almost severed ankle.

As we navigated through her memories, she shifted to another past life where she suddenly collided with a wooden stake.

Conclusion

Following the session, the woman reported a remarkable relief. The chronic tightness in her chest, along with the headaches and ankle pain, had vanished.

In her past life as a man, she had been struck on the head with a ball and chain, which we connected to her present-day headaches. The severe injury to her ankle in that life explained her current ankle pain.

Additionally, the trauma of running into a wooden stake in another life was linked to the tightness she felt in her chest. This session revealed a clear connection between past life experiences and present physical and mental ailments.

This leads us to consider whether these past life experiences might be inherited, passed down through generations. It poses an intriguing question: Are we possibly looking in the wrong direction for answers to our problems?

Could the experiences of our ancestors be influencing our physical and mental health in the present? And that we; Are Reliving Someone Else's Life?

Explain; Womb

Before your birth, you're already connected to your mother's emotions. If she experiences sadness, fear, worry, or anger, these feelings can imprint on you and may surface later in your life. What I mean to say is that the emotional challenges you face today might have their roots even before you were born.

It's important to know that it's not your fault. These emotional memories are stored in your subconscious right from the start. Then you're born, and it's like, "Welcome to Earth." In the first three years of life, ideally, your parents provide safety, nourishment, clothing, and lots of love. This is the best-case scenario, but unfortunately, not everyone has such a nurturing family environment. During these early years, you're learning about life, experiencing good and bad, happy and sad moments.

If you're of a certain age, you might start nursery school at three, which is a shift from the earlier practice of starting school at five. For a child, being away from family for the first time can be very difficult and even traumatic. At five years old, school starts, and this can be challenging too. School, however, is where learning and growth happen.

Until the age of seven, our brains are highly receptive, functioning in a Theta state that allows us to absorb information effortlessly, much like a sponge. After turning seven, there's a shift from the Theta state to Alpha and Beta brainwaves. During this phase, our development and learning processes evolve, with a strong emphasis on growth and learning through repetition.

In my practice, I often clarify to my clients that I'm not a medium. However, I introduce them to a thought experiment: imagine if there was a way to revisit and see the loved ones they have lost. Would they be interested in such a journey? To make this more personal, I review their notes to understand the significant people they've lost and whom they were close to. Although I can't explain how, I believe this experience is possible for them as well.

Next, I guide them through a visualisation exercise. I ask them to picture themselves at the top of a snow-covered slope, holding a snowball. As it's snowing, they roll the snowball down the hill. When they observe the snowball growing in size, I use this as a metaphor to help them see their life in a similar way — growing and accumulating experiences over time, much like the snowball.

When working with clients, my approach is focused and singular, searching for the root cause or concern that they are dealing with, regardless of the various reasons they may have sought help.

In my sessions with clients, my goal is always to identify the primary issue they are dealing with, regardless of the various reasons they might have come to you for.

Read that again. It is imperative that you understand this because clients will be coming to you with many problems, but there is only one thing you are searching for.

Consider a client who is struggling with unhappiness at the age of 42. This feeling of unhappiness might not have begun in their adult life but could have its roots in their mother's womb. Imagine that as a two-year-old, they encountered a situation that deepened this sense of sadness. Over the years, they continue to face instances that add to their unhappiness, bringing them to their current state.

The key point here is that their unhappiness isn't just about how they feel now; it's an accumulation of all the unhappy moments they've experienced, growing incrementally over time. It's like the snowball we talked about earlier, getting larger as it rolls down the hill. Each unhappy moment adds to this snowball, making it bigger and more significant.

Now give them three tests to do, and make it fun.

1. Clasp their hands together, index fingers separated, and get their fingers to lock together. Then, when their fingers lock together, ask them what they

want to achieve in their life; 99% of the time, they will give you the wrong answer.

Use this moment to guide them towards realising that the ultimate goal for many is actually happiness, not material achievements. This can be a revealing exercise to help them refocus on what truly matters in life.

2. Eye catalepsy. Get their eyes to stick using the Elman Induction:

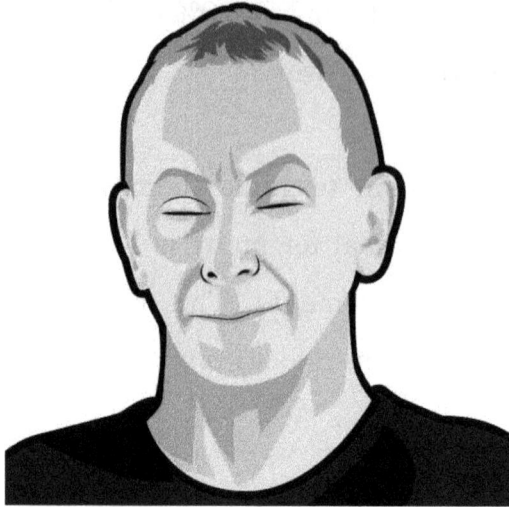

3. Right or left palm raised 6 inches from their face fingers together, focusing on the middle finger. Tell them their fingers will separate. Remember repetition; repeat again and again until they separate.

Do you want my help?

After the Pre-Talk, 99% of clients will say yes; they will now firmly believe that you can and will help them.

You have built trust, rapport and belief. When working with clients for the first time, they must believe in you. You are their last resort. The Pre-Talk works for everyone.

If you would like to see a complete Pre-Talk of a client I worked with, here is the link:

www.inheritedtherapy.com

The pre-talk I have created needs to be learned exactly as it is written. If you do this, people looking for help will be completely sure that you can help them in their tough times.

This pre-talk is special and works well for everybody. It's important to remember each word because this ensures consistency and effectiveness in conveying the message.

This approach has been tailored to resonate with a wide range of individuals, providing them with the confidence and assurance they need when they are going through difficult periods

Closing Thoughts

In conclusion, the key to making a strong impact with this introductory pre-talk lies in its precise memorisation and delivery.

By sticking to the script, you ensure that the message is consistently powerful and tailored to resonate with a diverse audience.

This approach not only builds trust among those seeking help but also establishes your credibility as a knowledgeable and empathetic guide.

Remember, the effectiveness of the pre-talk is in its careful design and the assurance it provides to those in need, making it a vital tool in your efforts to help others through their challenges.

Module 12: Inductions

1. Rapid Inductions (Dave Elman) · 3 – 5 Minutes

2. Progressive Relaxation Induction · 20 – 30 Minutes

3. Instant Induction · 30 – 60 seconds

Explaining an instant induction and how it works:

1. The 10 second hypnotist
2. The 60 second hypnotist
3. The hypnoidal five

Module 13: Explanation: Instant Induction:

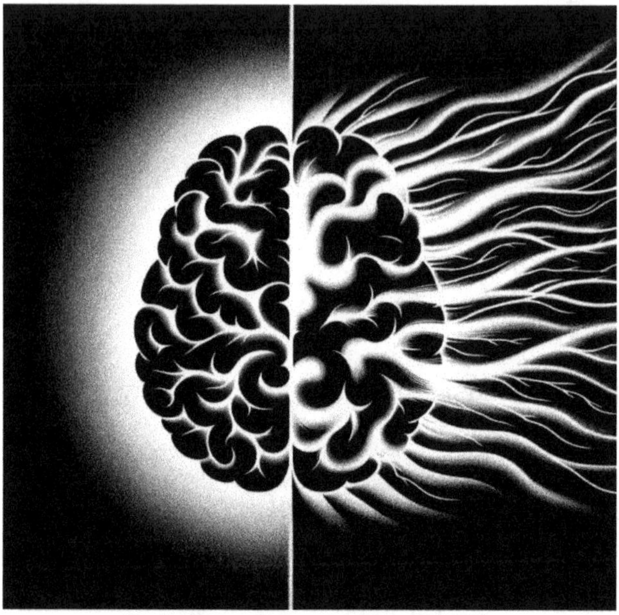

Subconscious state: Shock

Here's an abstract representation of the fight and flight response as described. The image illustrates the concept of the brain's reaction to shock and the brief window of opportunity for influence, transitioning from a heightened state of alertness to a more subdued subconscious state.

Fight and flight trigger a response to open up a window of opportunity (0.5 seconds) vulnerability open and accept a reasonable suggestion.

When a shock is given the mind spikes, 0.5 second window of opportunity then goes into subconscious and spikes up to consciousness UNLESS you keep talking.

As we wrap up the 13th module of this course, let's revisit the key lessons in a straightforward and concise manner:

This is related to hypnosis or psychological techniques that involve using a moment of shock or surprise to induce a state of heightened suggestibility. This concept is based on the idea that a sudden shock or surprise can momentarily disrupt the normal mental processes, creating a brief window of vulnerability or openness to suggestion.

Here's a breakdown of the process

Shock Induction: This involves presenting a sudden or unexpected stimulus that triggers a 'fight or flight' response in the subject. This response is a physiological reaction to perceived danger or stress.

Window of Opportunity (0.5 seconds): Immediately following the shock, there is a very brief period (around half a second) during which the person's usual mental defences or critical thinking processes might be bypassed or less active. This is seen as an opportunity for the hypnotist or practitioner to make a suggestion, sleep or deepener.

Mind Spikes and Subconscious Engagement: You mention that after this brief window, the mind 'spikes' possibly meaning that the person becomes more alert or defensive.

However, as the individual becomes more alert following the initial shock, continuous engagement or conversation might prevent the suggestion from effectively penetrating the subconscious.

Suggestion of Sleep and Fractionation: Suggesting sleep or relaxation can help guide the person back into a more suggestible, subconscious state. Fractionation, a technique in hypnosis, involves repeatedly bringing someone in and out of hypnotic trance, deepening the trance state with each iteration.

Deepener (Countdown from 10 to 0): This is a common hypnotic technique used to deepen the trance state.

The practitioner might count slowly from ten to zero, with each number suggesting deeper relaxation or immersion into the hypnotic state.

This process is complex and relies on an understanding of psychology and suggestibility.

It's important to note that such techniques should be used ethically and with the person's consent, as they involve manipulating mental and emotional states.

Closing thoughts

In summary, the technique you're referring to involves using a sudden shock to create a short moment when a person is more open to suggestions.

This brief period is seen as an opportunity for a hypnotist to influence the person's subconscious mind.

After the shock, techniques like suggesting relaxation and using repeated trance induction (fractionation) help deepen the hypnotic state.

It's important to use such methods ethically and with consent, as they involve influencing someone's mental state. Relates to The Hypnoidal Five.

Module 14: Hypnoidal Five:

Hello everyone, no matter where you are in the world — it's evening here in the UK as I write this — today we're diving into the fascinating topic of the "Hypnoidal Five", essential elements that influence our ability to enter hypnosis.

We're in this Module 14 of our learning journey, and I'm excited to share more with you. Let's start by revisiting a previous module, where we discussed ABS: Absorbing Attention, Bypassing the Critical Factor, and Stimulating the Unconscious Mind. These concepts are vital in understanding how we engage with the subconscious.

The Hypnoidal Five includes: 1) Fascination, such as eye fixation; 2) Boredom, characterised by monotony and repetition; 3) Confusion, including elements of shock and surprise; 4) Successive responses to suggestion; and 5) Loss of equilibrium.

These elements mix together to create a deep trance state. They're not just theoretical; they are used in practical inductions and instant inductions.

Let's delve into each element. First, eye fixation. It's about focusing attention, like staring into someone's eyes without blinking, leading them into trance. Then, boredom and repetition, which can manifest in activities like daydreaming or monotonous tasks, help to bypass the critical mind.

Confusion or shock creates a disruption, forcing the mind to quickly try to restore balance, which can be an opportune moment to induce trance. Successive responses to suggestions build a pattern of compliance, reinforcing the trance state. Lastly, loss of equilibrium, often used in shock inductions, disorients and makes the individual more susceptible to suggestion.

Understanding these elements is crucial for anyone practising hypnosis. Surprisingly, many hypnotists might not be aware of the Hypnoidal Five. As we progress, you'll see how these elements are not only scientifically backed but are also practical tools in inducing hypnosis.

Eye fixation (Focus)

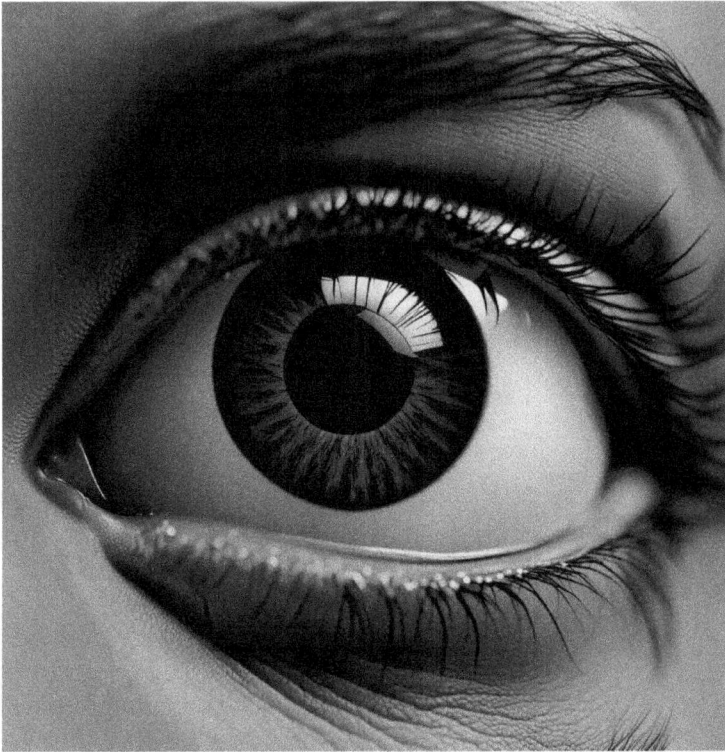

A.B.S. For example: cat playing with a string, flashing light, staring into space. Eye fixation at a point blocks out all the stimuli except what you are staring at. Eye fixation is an easy way to create fascination.

Tell them as they stare:

"You will block out all the stimuli around you, your eyes will become heavy and you will go into a trance."

Boredom, Monotony, Repetition

Progressive Relaxation. For example: assembly line, road hypnosis, daydreaming, doing two things at once.

Suggestions given in this state would take effect quickly

Confusion, Shock, Surprise

The mind and body tend towards equilibrium; when you throw the body out of equilibrium, it fights to get back into it.

Equilibrium is when you shock, confuse, and surprise the conscious mind, and it then focuses to find out what happened. The mind tries to resolve it very quickly to bring it back into equilibrium.

The "Yes" Set

Response to suggestion

Compounding; building a pattern of compliance by using several consecutive suggestions. Getting them to agree to say YES.

Yes

Yes

Yes

Loss of Equilibrium

- Shock
- Postural Sway
- Take them off balance
- Conscious mind focuses to get back into equilibrium

- Suggestion will take effect.
- Attention is absorbed.

Creating a Hypnoidal State Naturally

1. Fascination (Eye fixation)
2. Boredom, monotony, repetition
3. Confusion, shock, surprise
4. Successive response to suggestion (Yes Set)
5. Loss of equilibrium

Signs of Trance

1. Red or watery eyes
2. Rapid eye movement
3. Feeling warmer
4. Dilated pupils
5. Eyes rolling upwards
6. Moving and responding more slowly
7. More swallowing
8. Increased tear production
9. Deep sighs
10. Slow, uneven movements
11. Slower breathing

These signs indicate deep relaxation or a shift in consciousness.

On Closing

In summary, closing the eyes is a key aspect of entering a trance state as it aids in reducing distractions, focusing internally, enhancing relaxation, and facilitating deeper emotional and psychological processing.

Module 15: Analytical v. Non Analytical

People can be hypnotised differently and the approach should be customised for each person. Intelligence isn't a barrier to being hypnotised. There are generally two types of people: analytical and non-analytical.

To determine which type someone is, use suggestibility tests. It's rare to find someone who is completely analytical or completely non-analytical. In these tests, if someone follows instructions and reacts quickly, they're likely non-analytical.

The faster they respond, the more non-analytical they are. If their response is slower, the process continues differently.

CLASSIFICATION OF CLIENTS

Analytical:

The mind likes to keep itself busy and gets bored easily.

The conscious mind needs to be given tasks to allow access to the subconscious:

Non-Analytical:

The mind finds it easy to relax and switch off.

The conscious mind needs to be relaxed to allow access to the subconscious:

Physical Emotional or Emotional Physical:

Physical Emotional suggestable subjects are Non-Analytical:

- Psychosomatic internal physical problems
- Fear of flying
- Fear of heights
- Fear of closed spaces
- Procrastination
- Sales motivation
- Anxiety over exams
- Rejections
- Lack of confidence

Emotional Physical Suggestable subjects tend towards being Analytical:

- Psychosomatic external physical problems
- Depression
- Anxieties
- Indecisiveness
- Male and female sexual problems
- Lack of confidence
- Fear of contamination
- Fear of death
- Fear of loss of control
- Obsessive compulsive behaviour:

In general, emotional subjects suffer from more neurotic problems than the physical.

Module 16: Types of Inductions

Instant and Rapid Inductions

- Ambiguous Touch (Milton Erickson)
- Arm Bending
- Arm Drop
- Arm Raising
- Dave Elman Induction (Rapid)
- Eye Catalepsy
- Finger Snap
- Hand Clasp
- Hand Drop
- Handshake Interrupt (Confusion Induction)
- Hypnotic Gaze
- Magnetic Fingers
- Magnetic Hands

First and foremost, I must clarify that the concepts of the ten-second hypnotist and the sixty-second hypnotist, as well as H+, were not originally mine.

These techniques were imparted to me during a course I attended in Los Angeles in September 2011, led by the highly skilled hypnotist, Igor Ledochowski.[26]

The Ten-Second Hypnotist

1. Close your eyes; go into a trance.
2. Every time I touch you on the shoulder, arm, or forehead you go deeper.
3. Suggestions: Amazing Confidence; Easy to Lose Weight; Great Hypnotist.
4. Bring out– 1, 2, 3, eyes open.

The 60 Second Hypnotist

- H+ Intention
- Close your eyes
- Go deeper
- Boilerplate 1
- Sounds around you
- My voice will go with you wherever you go
- Chair of safety
- Suggestion
- Boilerplate 2
- Go deeper and quicker

---

[26] https://en.wikipedia.org/wiki/Led%C3%B3chowski

- Self-esteem (feeling good)
- Bring out

Eye closure, called catalepsy – challenge them, it is essential to bypass the critical factor.

Fractionation

(Eyes open, eyes closed; sends them deeper x 3)

- 10 x deeper
- Twice as deep
- Even deeper
- Physical Relaxation (Arm Drop)
- Mental Relaxation is a state of somnambulism (Amnesia)

The Hypnosis Game-Changer

One of the most important breakthroughs in hypnosis, which changed me into the Master Hypnotist that I am today, that will do the same for you.

Before we delve into the Elman induction, I'd like to take you back to a specific moment in time early in my hypnotism career.

Picture this: A client comes to my home for a session. She's agreed to be hypnotised, but as I begin, something unexpected happens. Despite my efforts, she just doesn't go under.

For over two hours, I'm there, working tirelessly to induce trance. Imagine the stress – sweat dripping, the pressure mounting. I knew that if I couldn't hypnotise her, it could spell the end of my confidence and possibly my career in hypnosis.

But I didn't give up. For three exhausting hours, I persevered until; finally, she slipped into a trance. It was a moment of both relief and realisation. I understood then that there had to be a more efficient way.

Driven by this experience, I embarked on a global journey in search of answers, seeking to master the art of hypnosis.

Finding the Key in Elman's Teachings

My quest for answers in the world of hypnosis led me to an unexpected source. It wasn't during my travels around the world, but through a book by Dave Elman entitled 'Hypnotherapy' that I found my breakthrough.

Reading this book was a revelation. It became like a bible to me, filled with Elman's techniques and insights.

The journey took an even more personal turn when my sons reached out to Dave Elman's son. In a generous response, he sent me a video of Dave Elman himself.

This was more than just a learning experience; it was a connection across generations, linking me directly to the wisdom of one of the great masters of hypnotherapy.

My journey into hypnosis took a significant turn when I learned about the Elman induction. This moment marked a crucial point in my exploration of hypnosis.

While I kept the core of this powerful method unchanged, I added my own twist to it a small yet significant tweak at the very end that amplified its effectiveness.

This refined approach has proven to be more potent, and now I can confidently say that it works on virtually everyone. It's not just learning a technique; it's about enhancing it to unlock its fullest potential.

Now imagine this · combining the unique pre·talk with the powerful Elman induction. Now, the only piece left to complete the puzzle is the Journey, made possible through the innovative The Loveday Method.

This trio of techniques isn't just a method; it's a pathway to unlocking the profound potential of the mind.

Read on to find the answers.

Elman Recovery Part 1: Dave Elman Induction[27]

Eye catalepsy (eyes locking)

"Take a deep breath in and as you breathe out close your eyes. Focus your full attention on your eyelids. Fully and completely. To the point that they become so relaxed, so heavy that they just won't work. Only when you're sure they won't work, test them, making sure they just won't work. Test them now. Stop trying. And send that quality of relaxation all the way down to your toes."

Fractionation (opening & closing eyes)

"In a moment I'm going to have you open and close your eyes, and as you do, you'll go 10x TIMES DEEPER. Eyes open. Eyes closing. Letting go.

---

[27] https://en.wikipedia.org/wiki/Dave_Elman

"In a moment I'm going to have you open and close your eyes, and this time you'll go TWICE AS DEEP. Eyes open. Eyes closing. Letting go. Dropping deeper and deeper. You're doing really well.

"In a moment I'm going to have you open and close your eyes, each time you do this you'll go ALL THE WAY. Expect it to happen. Allow it to happen. It'll happen easily and naturally. Dropping deeper and deeper"

Physical relaxation (arm dropping)

"In a moment I'm going to lift your hand up by your wrist (touched wrist). When I do it will become loose and limp. Let me do the work. Don't help me at all. When I lift your hand up and drop it down, it will send a wave of relaxation throughout your entire body (lift the hand up by the wrist and let it drop). All the way. All the way. Relax."

Amnesia (counting back from 100)

"Now, there are two ways the mind and the body relax. Physically and mentally. I'm going to show you how to relax mentally. In a moment I'm going to ask you to count back from 100 and I want you to push those numbers out of your mind. So by the time you get down to 98 or even sooner, let them fade away. I want you to start counting back from 100 out loud now. That's right. All gone. Have they gone?

If they continue counting, without stopping, you say, "Stop counting," then move onto the aphasia and say "Have they done?" at the end of that.

Aphasia (arm drop · leftover bits)

"In a moment I'm going to lift your hand up by your wrist (touch wrist) · when I do · I'll drop it down. The numbers will drop off the edge and you'll go even deeper. (Lift the hand up, drop it down and say:). "All gone. Have they gone?"

In this module we have learned about various techniques used in the Dave Elman Induction process for achieving trance or deep relaxation in hypnotherapy. These techniques include:

Eye Catalepsy (Eyes Locking): This involves instructing the individual to focus on their eyelids until they become so relaxed and heavy that they feel like they cannot open them. The person is then asked to test their eyelids to ensure they really cannot open them.

Fractionation (Opening & Closing Eyes): This is a process where the individual is asked to open and close their eyes several times. Each time, they are told that they will go deeper into relaxation or trance. The depth of trance is increased progressively with each opening and closing of the eyes.

Physical Relaxation (Arm Dropping): In this technique, the therapist lifts the individual's hand by the wrist and then drops it, signalling the body to release tension and relax deeply. This physical action helps facilitate a deeper state of relaxation.

Amnesia (Counting Back from 100): The individual is asked to count backwards from 100 and to let the numbers fade from their mind. This encourages mental relaxation and the fading of conscious thought processes, aiding in achieving a deeper state of trance.

Aphasia (Arm Drop · Leftover Bits): Similar to the physical relaxation technique, the therapist lifts and drops the individual's hand. This action is associated with the idea of letting any remaining conscious thoughts or numbers drop away, leading to an even deeper level of relaxation and trance.

These techniques are designed to guide an individual into a deeply relaxed state, where the mind is more receptive to suggestion and change. This state is often utilised in therapeutic settings to address various issues or to facilitate personal development and self-awareness.

On Closing

As we conclude this discussion on the Dave Elman Induction, it's important to recognise the significance of these techniques in the field of hypnotherapy. The Elman Induction is renowned for its effectiveness in creating a deep state of hypnosis quickly and reliably.

This method, characterised by eye catalepsy, fractionation, physical relaxation, amnesia, and aphasia techniques, demonstrates a sophisticated understanding of how to guide the mind into deep relaxation and heightened suggestibility.

In therapeutic settings, these techniques allow for a more profound engagement with the subconscious mind, enabling the therapist to work more effectively on various psychological and emotional issues. However, it's crucial to remember that such techniques should always be practised by trained professionals within a safe and ethical framework.

Understanding and respecting the power of these hypnotic techniques is key to their responsible and beneficial use. Whether in clinical therapy, personal development, or other applications of hypnotherapy, the principles of the Dave Elman Induction continue to influence modern practices and offer valuable insights into the human mind and its incredible capacity for change and healing.

Module 17: Boilerplate 1:

Sounds

"Now, you may hear various sounds and noises, outside noises, inside noises. Dogs barking, children laughing. But all these noises will drop you deeper and deeper."

Voice

"My voice will go with you wherever you go, and the meaning of everything I say will stay with you."

Safety

"Feel the chair and know you're safe at all times."

Closing Thoughts

As we conclude, it's essential to reflect on the journey we've taken together. The modifications to Module 17 have been crafted to provide a more immersive and comforting experience, focusing on the ambient sounds, the reassuring presence of the guiding voice, and the emphasis on safety and security. These elements are designed to create conducive environments for relaxation and introspection.

Remember, the effectiveness of such modules lies in their ability to resonate with the listener, offering a sense of peace, guidance, and security. It's about creating a space where the individual feels supported and at ease to explore their inner world.

The language used is just as important as the intention behind it, aiming to foster a deeper connection with the self and the surroundings.

As you move forward, whether it's in developing more content or in your personal endeavours, consider the power of words and the environment they create. The journey of self-discovery and relaxation is deeply personal, and facilitating that with care and thoughtfulness can make a significant difference.

Keep in mind the impact of a soothing voice, the reassurance of safety, and the role of ambient sounds in enhancing the overall experience.

Module 18: Fractionation and Deepeners:

DR OSKAR VOGT 1870 – 1959[28]

Opening and closing the eyes

"I want you to open your eyes and when you close them, you will go 10 x deeper."

---

[28] https://en.wikipedia.org/wiki/Oskar_Vogt

"In a few moments, I want you to open your eyes and then close them. Go twice as deep."

"In a few moments I want you to open them, close your eyes and go even deeper."

Black Jack Rule

- 1st Suggestion
- 2nd Suggestion reinforces 1st
- 3rd Suggestion reinforces 1st and 2nd

Compounding effect

- 15/21 repetitions of a suggestion for it to stick
- Suggestion – suggestion – suggestion

People need time to process information

Vogt Deepener

"In a moment, I'm going to count to 15. On the count of 10, your eyelids will just barely open. They'll become heavy, lazy, and droopy. As I keep counting, they'll become heavier and heavier. On a count of 15, your eyes will close down. Your head will tilt to the side and you'll drop even deeper."

The Vogt Deepener is another hypnotic technique used to enhance the depth of trance in an individual.

This technique is particularly effective in deepening the state of relaxation and suggestibility already achieved through previous induction methods. Here's a breakdown of the Vogt Deepener process:

Counting to 15: The hypnotist begins by informing the individual that they will count to 15. This sets up a structured and predictable framework for the deepening process.

Partial Opening of Eyelids at Count of 10: At the count of 10, the individual is instructed that their eyelids will open slightly. The description of the eyelids becoming "heavy, lazy, and droopy" suggests a state of relaxation that is so profound that it's challenging to keep the eyelids fully open.

Increasing Eyelid Heaviness: As the count progresses from 10 towards 15, the hypnotist emphasises the increasing heaviness of the eyelids. This suggestion aims to deepen the individual's sense of relaxation and trance. The increasing effort required to keep the eyelids open, juxtaposed against the growing heaviness, reinforces the individual's descent into a deeper state.

Eyes Closing and Deepening Trance at Count of 15:
Finally, at the count of 15, the individual is directed to close their eyes completely. The accompanying suggestion of the head tilting to the side and the individual dropping "even deeper" serves as a cue for a significant deepening of the trance state.

What have we learnt?

The Vogt Deepener in Detail

The Vogt Deepener is effective because it utilises the body's natural responses - in this case, the effort of keeping the eyelids open against growing heaviness - to amplify the hypnotic experience. This technique can be especially useful for individuals who respond well to structured, step-by-step guidance in their hypnotic journey.

As with all hypnotic techniques, the Vogt Deepener should be used by a trained and experienced practitioner, ensuring that it is applied safely and ethically within a therapeutic context.

Hello, everyone! Welcome to this Module where we're going to explore the concept of deepening hypnosis. Today's session includes an intriguing aspect called 'Fractionation'.

But before we dive in, let me share my screen with you — I'm getting quite adept at this!

We'll start by examining the idea of 'Fractionation' and its deepening effect. This concept was developed by Dr. Oscar Vogt, who lived from 1872 to 1959.

Remember our discussion about opening and closing your eyes to deepen the hypnotic state? It's fascinating. When you close your eyes after opening them, you descend ten times deeper into trance.

And with each repetition, you go even deeper. Let's understand why this happens. There's a fine line between the conscious and subconscious mind.

Using Fractionation, we navigate these states. By repeatedly opening and closing their eyes, the subject delves deeper each time into the subconscious realm. Now, onto the 'Blackjack Rule'.

This principle is about reinforcing successive suggestions. Each new suggestion strengthens the previous ones, creating a compounding effect. I'll illustrate this with an example.

Imagine hypnotising a woman to lower the radio volume each time I touch my nose, and a man to raise it each time I touch my neck.

As this cycle repeats, their responses become more immediate and pronounced, demonstrating how each suggestion builds upon the last.

This concept is important because it demonstrates the power of repetition in hypnosis — it usually takes about 15 to 21 repetitions for a suggestion to solidify.

This principle applies to various scenarios, such as quitting smoking or losing weight, where the mind gradually assimilates the suggestions.

Let's also consider the concept of 'deepening'. Why do we seek to deepen trance states? It's simple: the deeper the trance, the more receptive the mind becomes. I often use a countdown technique, where each descending number takes the subject deeper.

Physical cues, like touching the head or rotating the head, can also intensify this depth. The 'Void Deepener' is another fascinating technique I employ frequently. It involves opening and closing the eyes on command, each time sinking deeper into trance.

We'll do this in increments, using the Blackjack Rule, to reinforce the deepening effect. To wrap up today's module, let's briefly touch upon 'ABS' — Absorb Attention, Bypass the Critical Factor, and Stimulate the Unconscious Mind.

This concept, derived from the teachings of Igor Ledochowski. That's a lot to take in for one session! We'll pause here to allow you to absorb this information.

Our journey continues in the next Module, where we delve even deeper into the world of hypnosis. Thank you for joining today's session. I'll see you in the next module. Until then, take care and stay safe.

On Closing

The Dave Elman Induction and the Vogt Deepener are key techniques in hypnotherapy used to induce deep relaxation and suggestibility. These methods, through structured and progressive steps, effectively guide individuals into a hypnotic state, allowing for therapeutic work.

They highlight the importance of skilled practitioners in navigating these processes safely and underscore the profound impact of hypnotherapy in personal development and therapy.

Module 19: Post Hypnotic Suggestion

Post hypnotic suggestion is a suggestion given to be acted on at a later date:

Boilerplate 2

A suggestion made during hypnotic state to be carried out before awakening.

1. The next time you are with me, you will go deeper, quicker, faster.

2. Ask the question: Nod if you understand and accept this?

3. Heighten Self-Esteem: Over the next few days, you are going to feel better about yourself, etc.

Module 20: Bring Them Back

"In a moment, I'm going to count to 5. On the count of 5, your eyes will open and you'll feel energised and alert.

1 - You are beginning to emerge from hypnosis.

2- Feeling totally relaxed.

3 - Energy travelling from top of your forehead to the tips of your toes, feeling alive inside.

4 - Throat is clear, sinuses clear, kidney clear, head is clear, thoughts are so sharp.

5 - And eyes open, wide-awake, feeling amazing. When their eyes open, you say, "How are you doing!?"

Module 21: Regression

Two different forms of regression:

1. True Regression
2. Pseudo Regression

True Regression

Your subject experiences regression first hand, as if they are in it. They are experiencing events as if it is happening live. They can smell the smells, feel the emotions, they may even experience fear and anxiety.

Pseudo Regression

Experiencing the situation in the third person. As if they are sitting in the movie theatre watching them on screen and would not be feeling the actual emotions or pain.

Module 22: Complete Session: Regression

Start with The Elman Induction

Take a deep breath in and as you breathe out, close your eyes.

Focus your attention on your eyelids. Fully and completely. To the point that they become so relaxed, so heavy, that they just won't work.

Now, only when you're sure they won't work, I want you to test them, making sure they just don't work.

Test them now. Stop trying. And send that quality of relaxation all the way down to your toes.

Now, in a moment, I'm going to ask you to open and close your eyes, when you do, you'll go ten times deeper. Eyes opening. Eyes closing. Ten times deeper.

In a moment, I'm going to ask you to open and close your eyes again, when you do, you'll go twice as deep. Eyes opening. Eyes closing. Twice as deep. That's it. You're doing really well.

In a moment, I'm going to ask you to open and close your eyes one last time, and when you do, you'll go all the way. Expect it to happen. Allow it to happen. It'll happen easily and naturally. Eyes opening. Eyes closing. All the way. That's it, going deeper and deeper.

In a moment, I'm going to lift up your hand by your wrist. When I do, it'll become loose and limp. Let me do the work. Don't help me at all. I'm picking it up now, and as I drop it, you'll experience a wave of relaxation wash over your entire body.

Now, there are two ways the mind and the body relaxes; physically and mentally. I'm going to show you how to relax mentally. In a moment, I'm going to ask you to count backwards from 100 out loud. When I do, those numbers will just float out of your mind, so by the time you get to 98 or even sooner, they'll be gone. Let them go. Start counting out loud from 100 now.

That's it. Slowly. All the way. Have they gone?

Now, in a moment, I'm going to lift up your hand by your wrist and when I drop it, any bits that are left over will just drop off the edge and numbers completely gone you'll go even deeper. That's it. All the way, all the way.

Sounds Around you

Now, you may hear various sounds and noises. Inside noises. Outside noises. Dogs barking. Children laughing. But all those noises just drop you deeper and deeper.

The sound of my voice will go with you wherever you go and the meaning of everything I say will stay with you.

Feel the chair and know you're safe at all times.

Hand Raising

Now, I'd like you to focus your attention on your right arm for me. As you do, you'll notice it beginning to rise. Why? Because it represents all the obstacles in your life you've overcome. As it twitches and rises and lifts, you'll go even deeper. Twitching, rising, pulling, tugging, lifting higher and higher. That's it all the way.

That hand will continue to rise. And, as it does, your left arm will also continue to rise. This represents all the goals you've achieved in your life, as well as the goals you're going to achieve. And, as it rises, you feel a wave of relaxation and calmness wash over your entire body. Twitching, lifting, rising, pulling, tugging.

Now you'll notice both hands starting to come together like a magnet. Like uncontrollable forces, coming closer and closer together. When they touch, your hands will just drop into your lap and you'll go even deeper. That's it. All the way.

Vogt Deepener

Now, in a moment, I'm going to count to 15. By the time I get to 10, your eyelids will just barely open. They'll become heavy, lazy, and droopy. So by the time I get to 15, they'll close down, your head will tilt to the side and you'll drop even deeper.

Now, in a moment, I'm going to count to 15 again. By the time I get to 10, your eyelids will just barely open. They'll become heavy, lazy, and droopy. So by the time I get to 15, they'll close down, your head will tilt to the side and you'll drop even deeper.

Now, in a moment, I'm going to count to 15 one last time. By the time I get to 10, your eyelids will just barely open. They'll become heavy, lazy, and droopy. So by the time I get to 15, they'll close down, your head will tilt to the side and you'll drop even deeper.

Amazing. You're doing really well.

Regression Technique

Bring their issue to light, whether it's fear or sadness.

Aim to make them feel it more deeply by creating a clear image of their problem in their mind.

Use passion, excitement, and strong belief to do this.

Amplifying The Feeling:

Induce feeling: bring to the surface. Focus on the feeling, notice where it is in your body, and pay close attention as the feeling grows stronger.

This is about amplifying that feeling, painting a picture in the client's mind of their problem.

Use passion and enthusiasm and belief.

Use feeling as a bridge to regress in time, as you focus on this feeling it carries you back in time to the very first time you felt this emotion.

"Focus on the feeling you're experiencing. Can you feel it? Rate it on a scale from 1 to 10, where 1 is fine and 10 is terrible. If it's 5 or lower, try to intensify the feeling. Let's dive deeper into it, reliving the moment.

Now, rate your feeling on the scale.

Next, I'm going to gently touch your forehead. When I do, you'll travel back to the first time you felt this way. Remember, time is just a concept; it doesn't really exist. (Touch their forehead gently.)

Your there now:

- 'Is it daytime or night-time
- 'Are you inside or outside
- 'Are you with someone or on your own
- 'Who are you with

- 'How old are you

Get out of jail card if you can't think of what to say:
- 'What's happening now?

Get them to really experience and relive it.

'In a moment, I'm going to touch you on your forehead, you'll come back in the room with your eyes open, going deeper.' (Touch forehead.)

'Now there was a time before that when you felt safe, what were you doing 'And there was a time after that you felt safe, what were you doing?'

'In a moment, I'm going to touch you on your forehead, your eyes will close down and you're going to go back in time to before it happened, when you felt safe.' (Touch forehead.)

'Close your eyes. Go back to that memory, just before it happened. Take them to that safe place fast forward past the problem where they felt happy. Now bring them back in the room eyes open, going deeper.'

'You know something little NAME doesn't know, don't you? What is it? You survived. You got through it. Now, wouldn't it be great if little NAME knew what was going to happen, that he knew he was going to survive, and it wouldn't be a problem would it?'

Do you think that would help?

'In a moment, I'll touch you on your forehead, when I do, you'll to go back in time and tell him that he's going to get through it, that he's going to survive it tell how amazing he is that you will protect him.' (Touch forehead.)

'When you've explained everything to little NAME, nod your head for me.

'In a moment, I'm going to touch you on your forehead, your eyes will open and you'll go even deeper.'

"In a moment, I'm going to touch you on your forehead, your eyes will close and we'll go back to that memory, just before it happened, and everything is going to be OK." (Touch forehead.)

This time you're stronger.

You go back just before it happens, you're stronger, you face the problem, you don't run away from it, then you're back in the safe place. And open your eyes and your back in the room, going deeper.

Repeat 3 times it becomes less of a problem. (2 real. 1 cartoon.) Eyes open. Eyes closed.

Observer

In a moment, I'm going to touch you on your forehead and when I do, you'll enter a room with a TV with a remote control. This is a magical TV. It'll allow you to view as an observer

Get them to Imagine sitting in front of a TV with a remote in your hand. You turn it on and see memories of times when you were unhappy. But this time, you're just watching these memories, not feeling the old emotions.

You use the remote to fast-forward and rewind, focusing on the good moments. It's a way of learning from your past without being trapped in it, recognising that although the past can't be changed, you can choose to remember the positives and move forward.

Letting Go

Get them to open their eyes. Get them to close their eyes. 'This shouldn't have happened, should it? I want you to find somewhere you feel safe.'

When you've found that place, nod your head for me" (You grab a pillow for them, place it on their knees, hands on the pillow). Get them to find somewhere safe in their mind.

"Whoever is to blame will appear in front of you. Look into their eyes and tell me how you feel.' If it's someone they don't like, get them to tape that person to a chair, and release all those emotions by hitting the pillow, talking etc. (Keep working on it until they feel nothing for the person in front.)

Then say, "Tell me how you feel. When you look into this person's eyes, you feel nothing." Wait for a reply. "It isn't your fault, is it?"

Forgiveness

'I want you to forgive him/her. I want you to say this out loud, "I forgive you because my life is amazing etc." And forgiving you sets me free. When you've forgiven them and you look into their eyes and feel nothing, nod your head for me.'

Keep on repeating until they've talked to all the people they need to talk to, and forgiven all of them.

Then say, "Is there anyone else?" They'll say, "No." And you say, "There is. You invite this younger child into the room." Get them to forgive their younger self.

'Give them a hug, and something amazing is going to happen; the person you've lost is going to melt inside you, so that person is now with you. You feel happy, content, stronger than you've ever been.'

'Tell me the good that came out of this.' Reframe their perception to focus on the positive.

'On the count of 5, your eyes will open.'

Here's a breakdown of what we've learned from this approach:

Regression and Visualization: The technique involves guiding individuals to mentally regress to a time before a traumatic or difficult experience. This is intended to evoke a sense of calm and relaxation.

Communicating with Younger Self: The person is encouraged to communicate with their younger self, sharing insights and assurances that they survived the challenging experience. This can foster a sense of self-compassion and perspective.

Reframing the Experience: By revisiting the memory and altering the way it's perceived (e.g., watching it on a TV screen, reliving it with new knowledge), the person can detach from the intensity of the emotions initially associated with the event.

Emotional Release and Forgiveness: The technique includes an element of emotional release, where the individual is encouraged to express their feelings towards others involved in their memories, often leading to a process of forgiveness. This can be cathartic and may help in resolving pent-up emotions.

Self-Forgiveness: A crucial part of the process is guiding the individual to forgive themselves. This can be significant in overcoming self-blame and building self-compassion.

Positive Reframing: Finally, the focus is shifted to the positive aspects of the individual's life. This reframing helps in altering the narrative from one that's possibly dominated by past negatives to one that acknowledges and embraces the positives.

This approach combines elements of psychotherapy, particularly those found in cognitive-behavioural therapy and narrative therapy, where changing the narrative of one's experiences can lead to changes in emotions and behaviours.

However, it's important to note that such techniques should be facilitated by a trained professional, especially when dealing with deeply traumatic or sensitive memories. The effectiveness and appropriateness of these techniques can vary greatly depending on the individual and their specific circumstances.

Closing thoughts

The therapeutic approach described combines visualisation, emotional processing, and reframing past experiences. Key points to remember are:

Professional Guidance: Such techniques should ideally be conducted with a qualified therapist for safety and effectiveness.

Personal Variation: The impact of these methods can vary from person to person. Individual experiences and responses will differ.

Narrative Change: Altering how we perceive and narrate our past experiences can significantly affect our emotional wellbeing.

Emotional Healing: Acknowledging and processing emotions, especially through forgiveness and self-forgiveness, is crucial for emotional healing.

Positive Focus: Shifting focus to positive life aspects and personal growth can aid in overcoming negative past experiences.

Overall, this approach underscores the importance of guided therapeutic intervention, personalization of techniques, and the power of changing one's narrative for emotional healing.

In summary, this therapeutic approach is complex and multifaceted, requiring careful consideration and professional support. It has the potential to be a powerful tool for emotional healing and personal growth, but it should always be tailored to the individual's needs and handled with care.

Module 23: Complete session: Suggestion Therapy

Suggestion therapy example

"Take a deep breath in and as you breathe out, close your eyes.

"Focus your attention on your eyelids. Fully and completely. To the point that they become so relaxed, so heavy, that they just won't work.

"Now, only when you're sure they won't work, I want you to test them, making sure they just don't work.

"Test them now. Stop trying. And send that quality of relaxation all the way down to your toes.

"Now, in a moment, I'm going to ask you to open and close your eyes, when you do, you'll go ten times deeper. Eyes opening. Eyes closing. Ten times deeper.

"In a moment, I'm going to ask you to open and close your eyes again, when you do, you'll go twice as deep.

Eyes opening. Eyes closing. Twice as deep. That's it. You're doing really well.

"In a moment, I'm going to ask you to open and close your eyes one last time, and when you do, you'll go all the way. Expect it to happen. Allow it to happen. It'll happen easily and naturally. Eyes opening. Eyes closing. All the way. That's it, going deeper and deeper.

"In a moment, I'm going to lift up your hand by your wrist. When I do, it'll become loose and limp. Let me do the work. Don't help me at all. I'm picking it up now, and as I drop it, you'll experience a wave of relaxation wash over your entire body.

"Now, there are two ways the mind and the body relax; physically and mentally. I'm going to show you how to relax mentally. In a moment, I'm going to ask you to count backwards from 100 out loud. When I do, those numbers will just float out of your mind, so by the time you get to 98 or even sooner, they'll be gone. Let them go. Start counting out loud from 100 now.

"That's it. Slowly. All the way. 'Have they gone?

"Now, in a moment, I'm going to lift up your hand by your wrist and when I drop it, any bits that are left over will just drop off the edge and you'll go even deeper. That's it. All the way.

"Now, you may hear various sounds and noises. Inside noises. Outside noises. Dogs barking. Children laughing. But all those noises just drop you deeper and deeper.

"The sound of my voice will go with you wherever you go and the meaning of everything I say will stay with you.

"Feel the chair and know you're safe at all times.

"Now, I'd like you to focus your attention on your right arm for me. As you do, you'll notice it beginning to rise. Why? Because it represents all the obstacles in your life you've overcome. As it twitches and rises and lifts, you'll go even deeper. Twitching, rising, pulling, tugging, lifting higher and higher. That's it all the way.

"That hand will continue to rise. And, as it does, your left arm will also continue to rise. This represents all the goals you've achieved in your life, as well as the goals you're going to achieve. And, as it rises, you feel a wave of relaxation and calmness wash over your entire body. Twitching, lifting, rising, pulling, and tugging.

"Now you'll notice both hands starting to come together like a magnet. Like uncontrollable forces, coming closer and closer together. When they touch, your hands will just drop into your lap and you'll go even deeper. That's it. All the way.

"Now, in a moment, I'm going to count to 15. By the time I get to 10, your eyelids will just barely open. They'll become heavy, lazy, and droopy. So by the time I get to 15, they'll close down, your head will tilt to the side and you'll drop even deeper.

"Now, in a moment, I'm going to count to 15 again. By the time I get to 10, your eyelids will just barely open. They'll become heavy, lazy, and droopy. So by the time I get to 15, they'll close down, your head will tilt to the side and you'll drop even deeper.

"Now, in a moment, I'm going to count to 15 one last time. By the time I get to 10, your eyelids will just barely open. They'll become heavy, lazy, and droopy. So by the time I get to 15, they'll close down, your head will tilt to the side and you'll drop even deeper.

"Amazing. You're doing really well.

"You are relaxed now, and because you are so relaxed you begin to feel free from all tension, anxiety, and fear. You now realise that you are more confident and sure of yourself because you have taken the enormous first step to helping yourself.

"You begin to feel this strength from within, motivating you to overcome any and every obstacle that may stand in the way of your happiness, social life and home life.

"You will find that from this moment on you are developing more self-control. You will now face every situation in a calm and relaxed state of mind. Your thinking is very clear and sharp at all times

"You begin to feel that your self-respect and confidence are expanding more and more each day in every way. You now realise that in the past you felt helpless and overwhelmed and you are replacing that with confidence, strength and self-control. You are becoming a happy person now with a positive attitude towards life. You are succeeding now in all that you do and you have all the abilities necessary for success.

"Love is a natural state of being and you are naturally in a state of loving when you accept yourself and others totally and unconditionally. Realise that you do not have to approve anyone's actions, behaviour or appearance in order to willingly accept and love them. You feel warm and loving towards yourself and others.

"In a moment, I'm going to count to 5. On the count of 5, your eyes will open and you'll feel energised and alert."

1 - You are beginning to emerge from hypnosis.

2- Feeling totally relaxed.

3 - Energy travelling from top of your forehead to the tips of your toes, feeling alive inside.

4 · Throat is clear, sinuses clear, kidney clear, head is clear, thoughts are so sharp.

5 · And eyes open, wide-awake, feeling amazing. When their eyes open, you say, "How are you doing!?

Traditional Hypnotherapy (Scripts) vs Layered Hypnotherapy

Scripts don't deal with the root cause. They only deal with the individual surface problems, that's why there are so many different scripts.

Layered Hypnotherapy focuses on releasing the root cause of the problem, thus letting go of all the symptoms.

Module 24: Inductions for children: Development of Dr H.Bernheim[29] and Dr Liebault[30] technique

Two Finger Eye Closure Method

Fastest techniques for obtaining hypnosis for children.

This technique was first used 70 years ago. Results are obtained so quickly, it might be thought that the technique would induce only light hypnosis. This is not so. A better method has been devised for adults; there is no better technique for children than this.

Example, a child going to a dentist.

Make believe for a child using their imagination. Similar to Elman Induction, but child-friendly.

This is a passage taken from the book, Hypnotherapy, by Dave Elman rewritten in a different way.

---

29 https://www.encyclopedia.com/people/medicine/medicinebiographies/
hippolyte-bernheim
30 https://en.wikipedia.org/wiki/Ambroise-Auguste_Li%C3%A9beault30

Imagine Sarah, how you play with your toys, creating magical stories and adventures? In our dentist's office, we have a special adventure just for you, a game of make-believe that makes everything here feel like part of a story. If you join in this game, nothing we do will bother you.

You won't feel a thing because you'll be the hero of your own adventure. Would you like to become a part of this magical story? Great!

Let's start our adventure. First, I'll guide you to close your eyes gently, like we're starting a secret mission. I'll gently press your eyelids closed using my thumb and forefinger, like so. (**Carefully position your thumb and forefinger on the eyelids and softly pull them closed**). "Now, with all your heart and soul, pretend that you're unable to open your eyes.") Now, with all your might, pretend your eyes are locked shut by a magical force, so strong that no matter how hard you try, they won't open. That's your superpower for now. Give it a try – try to open them while holding onto that magic. It's tough, isn't it? That's the magic at work! With this magic, you can be anywhere you wish, even playing in your own world of toys, and you won't feel anything I do to help keep your teeth strong and healthy.

Module 25: Sleep Hypnosis - Dave Elman

What is sleep hypnosis? Hypnosis attached to sleep: Hypno–sleep

Let me just mention Dave Elman. I feel that he has not been given the credit he deserves for his achievement in hypnosis; he was truly an amazing hypnotist and a pioneer in hypnosis.

This is a passage taken from the book, Hypnotherapy, by Dave Elman. Rewritten in a different way.

I feel it is only right that, for this passage you are about to read, the credit should be given to this astounding hypnotist, Dave Elman.

Sleep Hypnosis that you can use for your children.

Whatever your child is suffering from, when your little one is fast asleep in bed, quietly go into the room and repeat this:

"This is your daddy (or mummy) speaking, you can hear me but you won't wake up. This is your daddy speaking, you can hear me but you won't wake up. You can hear me but you won't wake up . . . You can hear me but you won't wake up . . . You won't wake up . . . I'll know you're hearing me when the little finger that I'm touching begins to move."

(Touch the little finger gently, speak quietly and be persistent).

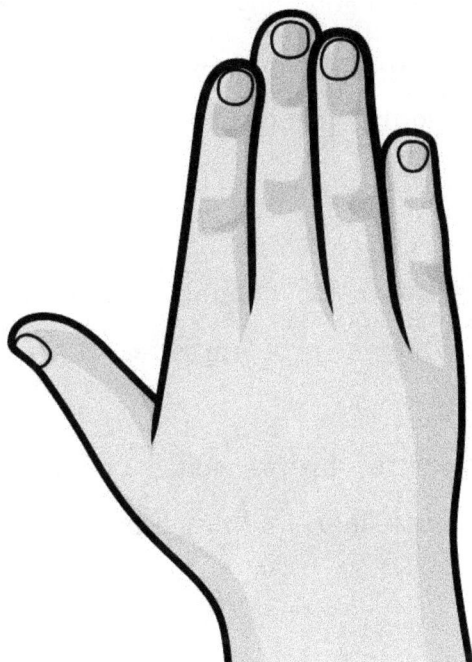

Once the little finger moves he or she can hear you and they are open to suggestions.

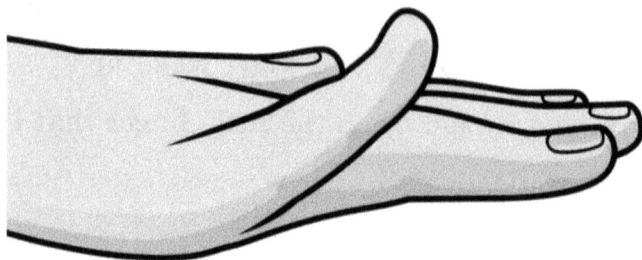

Example: For instance, let's assume the child is repeatedly naughty.

You will say "you are a good boy, your mummy loves you, your daddy loves you, and you love your mummy and daddy". Give only positive suggestions and repetition.

Repeat the suggestion for about one and a half minutes, no matter what the problem is.

This can help with biting nails, bedwetting, insomnia, being naughty, fear, and much more.

The finger has to move, as this will give you an indication that the child is listening and can hear you while asleep and respond to the suggestion given. And remember to be gentle, try not to wake them up, but if you do, it's not a problem just pretend to tuck them up in bed and go out of the room. And start again the next night.

We are conditioned up to the age of seven years old. We absorb information like a sponge in the Theta child's mind. We go from Theta to Alpha to Beta after seven years, when we advance, develop, and learn through repetition.

So while a child is sleeping, they are in delta, which is sleep mode, and by being persistent and getting their little finger to respond to you, they are open to suggestions and have gone from delta to theta, which means they are now in a very deep state of hypnosis.

Any suggestion given will take root in their subconscious mind and be acted upon. Do this for 30 days.

Module 26: Techniques

Techniques used for Inherited Therapy and The Loveday Method include:

1. Finding unconditional love.
2. The second chance.
3. The universe.
4. The library of life.
5. The magic key.
6. The magic crystal
7. The treasure map
8. Transport through time.
9. The secret pen.
10. The photograph.
11. The crystal ball.
12. Transfer of Energy
13. The book of life.
14. The white light.
15. A future representation of themselves.
16. The tunnel of time.
17. The release.

Module 27: Survey Literature

Survey literature by Alfred A Barrios, PhD, revealed the following recovery rates:

- Psychoanalysis - 38 per cent after 600 Sessions.

- Behaviour Therapy - 72 per cent after 22 Sessions.

- Hypnotherapy - 93 per cent after 6 Sessions.

- Geoffrey E Loveday creator of Inherited Therapy and the Loveday Method – 98% after just 6 sessions.

Now you can see how effective hypnotherapy and The Loveday Method is.

Module 28:The Universe:

Tell and Take

When working with a client, explain were you will take them, then take them there.

Please read that again.

Once you have them in a very deep trance, you will guide them on their spiritual quest for change. You will do six sessions; not one, but six. Each is a building block to the next stage.

I will do my best to help you understand the journey that you will take them on.

I will explain only one technique for the journey you will take them on. Each journey is different. For them, it is real; it is not fantasy. They are reliving the part of their ancestor's life that is causing a problem in their life today.

We do not use a script; you will be their guide. It is up to them to find the answers, not you!

Bring them into a very deep trance, then get them to imagine a set of stairs. Ask them if the stairs go up or down.

Under hypnosis, you will be talking to them, and they will be talking to you. You will get them to walk up the stairs, if they go up, from the 1st to the 10th.

At the top of the stairs, they will see a ball of light. You get them to enter the ball of light. Once there, you will guide them on their journey. They will rise, looking down at the earth, the trees, a distant mountain, and birds flying.

Get them to rise above the clouds, looking at the blue sky and the sun's warmth. Tell them, "You can feel the sun's warmth on your skin." Ask them questions.

Get them to rise further, out into the universe, seeing the millions of stars. They will then travel so fast they will see the circle of light, a doorway in time that they will travel through. The doorway will close behind them.

Now they will be in the emptiness, the quietness, the peacefulness, the stillness of time. This is a place from before we are born with all the memories passed down from our ancestors.

These past lives leave us, so when we are born, it's a new beginning, a new page, a new chapter in the book of life. But the memories are still there, memories we have forgotten. They are meant to be erased, and we are supposed to have no memory of them. But in life, things can sometimes bring those memories to the surface, and we start to feel unhappiness, depression, and anxiety, and we don't know why.

In this place of quietness and peacefulness, the vale has been lifted and can look back through time to the many lives of their ancestors, where the feelings causing a problem in life originated. As they look back through time, there will be one specific person they have a connection with, male or female. (They will see this person).

If they say female, ask them: "Is she young or old? What is she wearing? Are they old clothes? What year would you say she lives in? Is this someone you know or don't know?"

Get them to connect with this person; ask what they feel. Look into her eyes; what are you feeling right now?

The emotions will come to the surface, really amplifying these feelings.

Once they connect with them, they will realise that the unhappiness they are holding onto is the same. So you get them to release.

Have them repeat this: "We cannot live this life anymore; I cannot live your life, it is unfair for me to hold onto your pain, sadness, anger, and unhappiness, so I am giving it back to you now."

"As you say those words, see the dark energy leave you like a mist or smoke leaving you and entering the person in front of you. It's something they don't deserve to have. It has also been passed down to them as it was passed on to you, and you see this dark energy leave both of you, rising into the universe. Suddenly, a white ball of energy covers you both; you look into their eyes and ask them what they feel."

They will smile and say relief. The peace will feel like a weight has been lifted; you will then tell them to forgive them because it is not their fault. They are not to blame.

Then they will see another doorway open, like a circle of light. When they see this, ask them to nod their head; they will travel through and see an island in the distance. Ask them whether they have seen the island.

They will say yes; they will travel down to the island and get them to step out of the ball of light as it lands. Ask them if they are inside or outside, with someone or on their own.

Usually, they say outside, but nothing is set in stone; don't forget everyone is different. You are working on people, and you will act on the information given you then.

"Look up at the sky. Tell me what you see. Look down at the ground. Tell me what you see."

If they see sand, get them to see a path which leads inland with trees and flowers and notice the beautiful colours.

As they walk inland, everything will change colour to the most beautiful reds they have ever seen, the trees, the flowers, grass, and shades of red. Get them to see the red as they walk. The colour red enters their crown, travels down their spine to the base of their spine, recharges the root chakra, and a beam of light travels out of their body. Get them to see the light. They will.

As they walk, everything changes colour to the most beautiful orange; get them to breathe in; it enters the crown, travels down their spine, rests two inches above the root chakra, the sacral, and a very bright beam of light travels out. Again, get them to see it.

They walk; like life itself, everything changes from orange to yellow, the most beautiful yellow they have ever seen. Breathing it in, it enters the crown, travels down their spine, and pushes out a beautiful beam of light through their solar plexus, recharging life's energy centres.

Again, carrying on walking, everything changes colour to the most beautiful green, representing unconditional love. Breathing it in through the crown, it travels down the base of their spine and shoots out through the centre of their chest, the heart chakra.

Carry on walking; it changes again from green to light blue/turquoise, enters the crown, travels down the base of the neck, and pushes out through their throat as the throat chakra. These beams of light are becoming progressively more substantial.

Carry on walking, and it changes again from light blue to indigo, enters the crown, and travels down to the back of the head. Pushing through the brow, it opens up the third eye chakra.

Carry on walking, and again it changes, from indigo to violet; entering the crown, this light recharges every chakra in the body's life force, becoming much more substantial.

You will then say, "You have the power to change the world; I will prove it."

As they carry on walking, beams of light travel out of their body to form the most beautiful rainbow. Get them to see it.

Then say there is a "pot of gold" at the rainbow's end. For everyone, it is different. It can be a treasure, a letter, a stone, intuition, or a person, but only they will understand the meaning. So, your job is to listen; they have to find the answers, not you.

Then get them to find the end of the rainbow; when they find it, ask them what the message that they have found is. (This is where you have to think on your feet.)

Once they have found the answers they have been searching for, get them to go back to the ball of light. They will travel high into the sky, opening another doorway of light that will appear, and they will travel through the doorway, which will close behind them.

They will be in the emptiness, quietness, and peacefulness; another doorway will open up, and they will travel through, and the doorway will close. They will see millions of stars and then travel back until they see the earth. Then, when they think of the problem and go beyond it, they will realise they've so much more to live for more than they can imagine.

Then something magical will happen. Every star in the universe will shoot bolts of light and love into them.

Then, as they grow brighter and brighter, they become a star in the universe, connected to everything.

They float back to earth, travel down, and step out of the light, walking back down the stairs and counting from 1 to 5. The session ends.

If you would like to watch a complete session of a client who I worked on being taken to the universe, here is the link:

https://www.inheritedtherapy.com

PART FOUR

The Journey

Here is where the magic begins. There are three questions you need to ask:

1. If you had one wish, what would you ask?
2. How would it change you?
3. What would you change about yourself if you could go back in time?

When you ask three questions, the first question works on the left brain; the second question works on the right brain and starts to think inwardly; the third question also works on the right brain. Then they start to look inside themselves for the answers.

When you ask these questions, you will notice how their eyes look down and how the movement of their bodies changes. Now the truth comes out.

This story is to be told to the client during the pre-talk or under hypnosis.

The Genie in the Lamp

Aladdin was walking in the desert; he noticed something glowing in the sand. He stops to find a lamp and places it in his bag. An hour or so later, he stops for a drink.

He remembers the lamp he found an hour or so before he takes it out of his bag. Thinking he will sell it in the market, he notices a speck of dust, and as he wiped it clean, a genie pops out and grants Aladdin three wishes.

If you were given three wishes, what would you wish for? Only three wishes; so don't waste them.

Yet we have one life and waste the things that matter the most.

1. Now this story reminds me of life. The past teaches us everything about who we are and what we have become. Everything in life is a test - a challenge - and it guides us on our journey in life.

The past is how we learn.

2. Now, this moment is a gift. Have you heard the saying "live in the moment"?

You will never have it again; we cannot buy time no matter how much money we have. So don't waste a single moment of your life · It's too precious; once those seconds are gone, they are gone forever.

That's another second and another – in the blink of an eye, gone. So live life to the fullest. So be happy, find that passion for living, and get excited again.

3. Now tomorrow is a new beginning, a new start. It is like a film, a book, or a story, all about you.

If you want to be happy, write it down; if you want success too, write it down; and if you want to change, write it down and believe it. Make your life have meaning.

You see, you don't have three wishes; you have millions of wishes; they've just not been written yet.

As the hypnotist, you ARE the genie from the lamp. Remember to believe in yourself and whoever comes to see you; always remember that you can help them, no matter the problem.

"Your mind is so powerful; never doubt your ability and never be drawn into their world."
                              - Geoffrey E. Loveday

Suggestions take place on two levels; one is Mental (Fantasy); another one is Physical (Reality).

Now the magic begins, as does the "Journey".

You have to believe that you can take them anywhere in their mind, and you will, using these techniques I am about to share with you. You will be amazed at the results of regression suggestions and, of course, The Loveday Method.

Now the art of this technique is to guide them to find the root cause of the problem and find from where it first originated.

To take them into the past, where they will relive a moment in First Person. It will become apparent to them that the root of it all was just a trigger for something they have had all their life. Something is passed down not only from one ancestor but also from many ancestors, and they are reliving their lives.

Remember, the mind does not know the difference between what is real and what is not.

"Imagination is more important than knowledge."
- Albert Einstein.

How to access a part of the brain to navigate through the mind to relive your ancestors' life.

Module 29: Working with adults

Let me take you on this magical journey

On these magical journeys, you will take your clients on a spiritual quest to find themselves and become the person they are meant to be. They will realise that they are not alone, it is not their fault, and they are not to blame. And they will free themselves from the shackles and chains holding them back.

Every client is unique. You are just a guide, and they must find the answers themselves. Each journey is tailor-made for them.

There is a way to access a specific part of the brain to navigate the mind and relive our ancestors' lives. Let us begin.

This new approach uses suggestion, regression The Loveday Method and Inherited Therapy together.

The Pre-talk

In the initial discussion, we will conduct a thorough review of the client's history. It will become evident during this pre-talk that the emotions they've been holding onto existed well before their birth.

After this pre-talk, if you feel this approach aligns with your needs and you wish to proceed with our help, we will arrange appointments accordingly. If not, there will be no charge.

The journey then commences, spanning over six weeks with one session each week.

Session 1:

Regression through time

In our initial session, we focus on exploring the individual's current mental state and their memories. This is done through a gentle regression technique that helps surface emotions, enabling them to confront their issues directly.

During this session, participants experience a profound sense of unconditional love. This is achieved by guiding them through significant early life events —

their first steps, first birthday, the moment of birth, and the initial loving embrace of their mother.

Emphasis is placed on the interconnected health of the mother and child, exploring the maternal bond from the womb itself. This journey allows the individual to deeply empathise with their mother's experiences and emotions, even before their birth.

It's important to note that this experience feels incredibly real to participants. They vividly see and hear everything as if reliving those moments. Following these intense recollections, the session shifts to recalling happier times in the participant's life.

Addressing the loss of a family member is also a crucial part of this process, as such losses can profoundly impact a person's life. The session guides them through these memories, allowing them to release pent-up emotions and find closure. However, it is essential to clarify that I am not a medium, but rather a guide in this journey.

After bringing the participant out of hypnosis, it's common for the first session to be emotionally charged.

In the 48 hours that follow, the mind actively processes and releases these emotions, often leading to noticeable changes. However, individual experiences may vary, and no guarantees can be made about the outcomes. While results differ from person to person, the results can also be mind–blowing.

Session 2:

The universe

You will take them on an enchanting journey transcending time and space, entering a serene universe. Here, the shroud of time dissipates, allowing them to observe their ancestors and uncover the root of past issues, bringing about their release. Following this, you will guide them to a mystical realm where they will activate each chakra in their body.

As the session concludes and they emerge from hypnosis, they will find the transformations experienced to be quite astounding.

Session 3:

The Akashic Library

You guide them on an extraordinary voyage to the Akashic Library, the Library of Life. Within this library, you will navigate through time, leading them on a quest where they can inhabit the experiences of a relative, be it a grandparent, great-grandparent, uncle, or aunt.

This immersive journey helps them confront and release any lingering traumatic memories that have been the root of their issues.

Afterwards, you will return with them to the library, a place where they can uncover the answers they seek. As a guide, your role is not to provide solutions, but to facilitate their own discovery.

The journey concludes as the hypnosis session comes to an end.

Session 4:

Quest in search of a treasure map

Your upcoming adventure promises to be an extraordinary one. You will embark on a quest in search of a treasure map, journeying across time. In this experience, you will vividly live through a moment as one of your ancestors, long before your birth, allowing you to release and let go. The details of this journey are vast and mysterious, adding to the magical essence of the experience.

Session 5:

The Adventure of Change and the Lost Key

You will guide them through a journey across time and space in pursuit of a key that has been lost. Following this, the journey takes a deeper turn as you transport them back to a pivotal moment in their past, an event that lies at the core of a current issue in their life.

Session 6:

The magical crystal:

You will take them on a quest to discover the magic crystal, a mystical gem that unlocks the secrets of their past. This is an adventure they must experience, leading to the release of their long-held emotions. It is here that the enchanting journey of life truly begins.

Module 30: Working with children

I mentioned six sessions; well, there are seven. The first session is the pre–talk. This session is free.

During the pre–talk, a comprehensive discussion of the client's past will take place. After hearing the pre–talk, it will become abundantly clear to you that the emotions you have been clinging to were present long before you were even born.

Following the pre–talk, if you believe it is for you and you want our help, appointments will be scheduled; otherwise, there will be no charge.

When working with children up to the age of 18 a parent will be present.

And so the journey begins. Over six weeks, one session per week.

There you have it, the help your children desperately need is here.

For information visit these sites.
https://www.inheritedtherapy.com
https://www.liverpoolhypnosis.co.uk

The Journey

Session 1

In the first session we work on the human mind of the present and the memories, by a gentle approach using regression, the child's emotions will be brought to the surface to face the problem.

During that session they will be shown unconditional love by taking them back to the first time they walked, their first birthday, when they were born when their mum is healthy the child is healthy and the mother held the child in her arms for the first time, they will be taken into the mother's womb they will feel a connection of what the mother was going through and the feelings she felt well before the child was born.

You have to understand that it feels real. They see and hear everything. After that, they will be taken to happy times in that child's life.

Now depending on the age of the child ranging from 11 to 18 years, also with the parent's consent, when a child has lost a family member, it can have a huge effect on the child as they go through life. They can be taken to see them, release these feelings and give them back. I must emphasise that the parent has to give their permission. I am not a medium, I am a guide. The parent will always be present.

They are then brought out of hypnosis. The first session can be emotional. During the 48 hours following the session, the mind processes and releases, and after that, you will see changes. However, every child is different. And I must stress, no guarantee can be given. The results may vary from child to child. But the results can also be mind–blowing.

Session 2

Your child will be taken on a magical adventure through time and space into the universe, transported to a place of calmness where the veil has been lifted and they can look back through time and see past ancestors, where the problem originated, and release them. They will then be taken to a magical place where we will open up all the chakras in the body.

The session ends; brought out of hypnosis. The changes can be quite remarkable.

Session 3

Wow, what a journey your child will go on now! They are taken to the Akashic library, The Library of Life, and what a journey it is. In this library, they will be transported through time to be able to lead them on an adventure where they can experience something from the perspective of an ancestor such as a grandparent, great–grandparent, uncle, or aunt, thereby releasing whatever traumatic memories they may be clinging to, which has been the cause of the problem they have been holding onto and give them back.

They will be then taken back to the library where they will find the answers they need. I am only a guide. I do not offer them the solutions; they must discover them on their own.

The hypnosis session ends.

Session 4

The next adventure your child will go on is quite surreal. They will be taken on a journey where your child will search for a treasure map. Again they will be transported through time, where they will live a moment in first person as an ancestor many years before they were born. And be able to let go. Of course, there is a lot more but that is the magic.

Session 5

An adventure of change, and the lost key. Next, your child will go on an adventure across time and space to retrieve the misplaced key. After that, they will be transported back in time to a significant event in their past that is the source of a problem in their present life.

Session 6

The magical crystal. Your child will go on a quest to find the magic crystal. A magical gem is the key to your child's past and awaits them on an adventure they must undertake. Their pent–up emotions will finally be released.

And so the magic of life begins.

The Ancestral Journey

While writing this book, I realised that, whether you are an experienced hypnotist or a beginner, it may be challenging to learn from the writings in a book. I have done my best to show you some of the techniques, but you can only learn so much from reading. You have to experience it.

So, if you are interested in being trained, now is the time. These techniques are NEW.

Getting in at the beginning of The Loveday Method is the way forward, entering a unique approach to hypnotherapy today.

I know because I created it.

The Loveday Method is one of my newest approaches to helping people overcome many problems and symptoms that are holding them back from living a happy and fulfilling life.

Conclusion

Now, if you are at this point in the book, you will have read the stories of just a few of the people I have worked on and how it has changed their lives and looked into the research of the respected scientist who believes genetics can be passed down from one generation to the next.

I hope you realise that many of today's problems existed before we were born. And that we are living someone else's life. And taking on their pain as if they were our own.

Words of Wisdom, from me to you.

There are times in our life when we want to take a chance. We say to ourselves I am not ready; I'll wait. No point in delaying; there is never a right time.

WE ARE NEVER READY.

The only chance we have to reach our true potential is when we rise to life's challenges. I hope you realise that you are now on the cusp of a huge discovery. This is an entirely new way of thinking.

I want to introduce you to a new world, a world of endless wonders and endless possibilities. If you're an aspiring hypnotherapist or looking for a new career and want to become certified in The Loveday Method, visit this page to get started.

https://www.inheritedtherapy.com

Please contact me through: www.inheritedtherapy.com

How To Reverse Disease In The Body?

The Loveday Method
Part 6

Do your thoughts have the power to heal you? Or can your thoughts fuel disease?

Just suppose you could reverse disease in the body.

This is an interesting concept. So get my next book to find the answers. Due out toward the end of 2024

Bibliography

1. Yehuda, R., Daskalakis, N.P., Lehrner, A., Desarnaud, F., Bader, H.N., Makotkine, I., Flory, J.D., Bierer, L.M. and Meaney, M.J. (2014). Influences of Maternal and Paternal PTSD on Epigenetic Regulation of the Glucocorticoid Receptor Gene in Holocaust Survivor Offspring. American Journal of Psychiatry, 171(8), pp.872–880.

2. https://www.nobelprize.org/prizes/medicine/2012/press-release/Immortality. Cell Stem Cell, 11(6), pp.748–750.

3. Surani, M. Azim (2012). Cellular Reprogramming in Pursuit of

4. Yehuda, R., Daskalakis, N.P., Lehrner, A., Desarnaud, F., Bader, H.N., Makotkine, I., Flory, J.D., Bierer, L.M. and Meaney, M.J. (2014). Influences of Maternal and Paternal PTSD on Epigenetic Regulation of the Glucocorticoid Receptor Gene in Holocaust Survivor Offspring.

5. Morris, A.S., Silk, J.S., Steinberg, L., Myers, S.S. and Robinson, L.R. (2007). The Role of the Family Context in the Development of Emotion Regulation. Social Development, [online] 16(2), pp.361–388.

6. https://en.wikipedia.org/wiki/Donald_O._Hebb.

7. https://en.wikipedia.org/wiki/The_Sinking_of_the_Lusitania

8. https://en.wikipedia.org/wiki/Milton_H._Erickson

9. https://en.wikipedia.org/wiki/Martin_Theodore_Orne

10. LeCron, Leslie M. (1892-1972) | Encyclopedia.com

11. https://en.wikipedia.org/wiki/George_Estabrooks

12. https://en.wikipedia.org/wiki/Josephine_R._Hilgard

13. https://en.wikiquote.org/wiki/William_James

14. https://en.wikipedia.org/wiki/Franz_Mesmer

15. https://en.wikipedia.org/wiki/Amand-Marie-Jacques_de_Chastenet,_Marquis_of_Puységur

16. https://en.wikipedia.org/wiki/James_Braid_(surgeon)

17. https://www.ukhypnosis.com/2019/07/25/beginners-guide-to-the-history-of-hypnosis-timeline/

18. https://en.wikipedia.org/wiki/James_Esdaile

19. https://en.wikipedia.org/wiki/Sigmund_Freud

20. https://en.wikipedia.org/wiki/Milton_H._Erickson

21. https://www.inheritedtherapy.com

22. https://www.sciencedirect.com/topics/nursing-and-health-professions/abreaction#:~:text=Clinically%2C%20Freud%20initially%20worked%20using,%E2%80%93%20the%20%27cathartic%20method%27.

23. Wolynn, M., 2017. It Didn't Start with You. Penguin Publishing Group, p.125.

24. Shadrach, J.L., Gomez-Frittelli, J. and Kaltschmidt, J.A. (2021).

25. "Proprioception Revisited: Where do we Stand? Current Opinion in Physiology."

26. https://en.wikipedia.org/wiki/Led%C3%B3chowski

27. https://en.wikipedia.org/wiki/Dave_Elman

28. https://en.wikipedia.org/wiki/Oskar_Vogt
29. https://www.encyclopedia.com/people/medicine/medicine-biographies/hippolyte-bernheim

30. https://en.wikipedia.org/wiki/Ambroise-Auguste_Li%C3%A9beault

www.ingramcontent.com/pod-product-compliance
Lightning Source LLC
Chambersburg PA
CBHW071544210326
41597CB00019B/3116